Chicago Cubs 2021

A Baseball Companion

Edited by Steven Goldman and Bret Sayre

Baseball Prospectus

Craig Brown, Associate Editor
Robert Au, Harry Pavlidis and Amy Pircher, Statistics Editors

Copyright © 2021 by DIY Baseball, LLC.
All rights reserved

This book or any part thereof may not be reproduced or transmitted in any form or by any means, electronic or mechanical, including photocopying, recording, or by any information storage and retrieval system, without permission in writing from the publisher.

Limit of Liability/Disclaimer of Warranty: While the publisher and the author have used their best efforts in preparing this book, they make no representations or warranties with respect to the accuracy or completeness of the contents of this book and specifically disclaim any implied warranties of merchantability or fitness for a particular purpose. No warranty may be created or extended by sales representatives or written sales materials. The advice and strategies contained herein may not be suitable for your situation. You should consult with a professional where appropriate. Neither the publisher nor the author shall be liable for any loss of profit or any other commercial damages, including but not limited to special, incidental, consequential, or other damages.

Library of Congress Cataloging-in-Publication Data:
paperback
ISBN-13: 978-1-950716-33-3

Project Credits
Cover Design: Ginny Searle
Interior Design and Production: Amy Pircher, Robert Au
Layout: Amy Pircher, Robert Au

Baseball icon courtesy of Uberux, from https://www.shareicon.net/author/uberux

Ballpark diagram courtesy of Lou Spirito/THIRTY81 Project, https://thirty81project.com/

Manufactured in the United States of America
10 9 8 7 6 5 4 3 2 1

Table of Contents

Statistical Introduction v

Part 1: Team Analysis
Performance Graphs 3
2020 Team Performance 4
2021 Team Projections 5
Team Personnel 6
Wrigley Field Stats 7
Cubs Team Analysis 9

Part 2: Player Analysis
Cubs Player Analysis 14
Cubs Prospects 87

Part 3: Featured Articles
Cubs All-Time Top 10 Players 97
    by Matthew Trueblood

A Taxonomy of 2020 Abnormalities 103
    by Rob Mains

Tranches of WAR 109
    by Russell A. Carleton

Secondhand Sport 115
    by Patrick Dubuque

Steve Dalkowski Dreaming 119
    by Steven Goldman

A Reward For A Functioning Society 123
    by Cory Frontin and Craig Goldstein

Index of Names 127

Statistical Introduction

Sports are, fundamentally, a blend of athletic endeavor and storytelling. Baseball, like any other sport, tells its stories in so many ways: in the arc of a game from the stands or a season from the box scores, in photos, or even in numbers. At Baseball Prospectus, we understand that statistics don't replace observation or any of baseball's stories, but complement everything else that makes the game so much fun.

What stats help us with is with patterns and precision, variance and value. This book can help you learn things you may not see from watching a game or hundred, whether it's the path of a career over time or the breadth of the entire MLB. We'd also never ask you to choose between our numbers and the experience of viewing a game from the cheap seats or the comfort of your home; our publication combines running the numbers with observations and wisdom from some of the brightest minds we can find. But if you *do* want to learn more about the numbers beyond what's on the backs of player jerseys, let us help explain.

Offense

We've revised our methodology for determining batting value. Long-time readers of the book will notice that we've retired True Average in favor of a new metric: Deserved Runs Created Plus (DRC+). Developed by Jonathan Judge and our stats team, this statistic measures everything a player does at the plate–reaching base, hitting for power, making outs, and moving runners over–and puts it on a scale where 100 equals league-average performance. A DRC+ of 150 is terrific, a DRC+ of 100 is average and a DRC+ of 75 means you better be an excellent defender.

DRC+ also does a better job than any of our previous metrics in taking contextual factors into account. The model adjusts for how the park affects performance, but also for things like the talent of the opposing pitcher, value of different types of batted-ball events, league, temperature and other factors. It's able to describe a player's expected offensive contribution than any other statistic we've found over the years, and also does a better job of predicting future performance as well.

The other aspect of run-scoring is baserunning, which we quantify using Baserunning Runs. BRR not only records the value of stolen bases (or getting caught in the act), but also accounts for all the stuff that doesn't show up on the back of a baseball card: a runner's ability to go first to third on a single, or advance on a fly ball.

Defense

Where offensive value is *relatively* easy to identify and understand, defensive value is … not. Over the past dozen years, the sabermetric community has focused mostly on stats based on zone data: a real-live human person records the type of batted ball and estimated landing location, and models are created that give expected outs. From there, you can compare fielders' actual outs to those expected ones. Simple, right?

Unfortunately, zone data has two major issues. First, zone data is recorded by commercial data providers who keep the raw data private unless you pay for it. (All the statistics we build in this book and on our website use public data as inputs.) That hurts our ability to test assumptions or duplicate results. Second, over the years it has become apparent that there's quite a bit of "noise" in zone-based fielding analysis. Sometimes the conclusions drawn from zone data don't hold up to scrutiny, and sometimes the different data provided by different providers don't look anything alike, giving wildly different results. Sometimes the hard-working professional stringers or scorers might unknowingly inflict unconscious bias into the mix: for example good fielders will often be credited with more expected outs despite the data, and ballparks with high press boxes tend to score more line drives than ones with a lower press box.

Enter our Fielding Runs Above Average (FRAA). For most positions, FRAA is built from play-by-play data, which allows us to avoid the subjectivity found in many other fielding metrics. The idea is this: count how many fielding plays are made by a given player and compare that to expected plays for an average fielder at their position (based on pitcher ground ball tendencies and batter handedness). Then we adjust for park and base-out situations.

When it comes to catchers, our methodology is a little different thanks to the laundry list of responsibilities they're tasked with beyond just, well, catching and throwing the ball. By now you've probably heard about "framing" or the art of making umpires more likely to call balls outside the strike zone for strikes. To put this into one tidy number, we incorporate pitch tracking data (for the years it exists) and adjust for important factors like pitcher, umpire, batter and home-field advantage using a mixed-model approach. This grants us a number for how many strikes the catcher is personally adding to (or subtracting from) his pitchers' performance … which we then convert to runs added or lost using linear weights.

Framing is one of the biggest parts of determining catcher value, but we also take into account blocking balls from going past, whether a scorer deems it a passed ball or a wild pitch. We use a similar approach—one that really benefits from the pitch tracking data that tells us what ends up in the dirt and what doesn't. We also include a catcher's ability to prevent stolen bases and how well they field balls in play, and *finally* we come up with our FRAA for catchers.

Pitching

Both pitching and fielding make up the half of baseball that isn't run scoring: run prevention. Separating pitching from fielding is a tough task, and most recent pitching analysis has branched off from Voros McCracken's famous (and controversial) statement, "There is little if any difference among major-league pitchers in their ability to prevent hits on balls hit in the field of play." The research of the analytic community has validated this to some extent, and there are a host of "defense-independent" pitching measures that have been developed to try and extract the effect of the defense behind a hurler from the pitcher's work.

Our solution to this quandary is Deserved Run Average (DRA), our core pitching metric. DRA seeks to evaluate a pitcher's performance, much like earned run average (ERA), the tried-and-true pitching stat you've seen on every baseball broadcast or box score from the past century, but it's very different. To start, DRA takes an event-by-event look at what the pitchers does, and adjusts the value of that event based on different environmental factors like park, batter, catcher, umpire, base-out situation, run differential, inning, defense, home field advantage, pitcher role and temperature. That mixed model gives us a pitcher's expected contribution, similar to what we do for our DRC+ model for hitters and FRAA model for catchers. (Oh, and we also consider the pitcher's effect on basestealing and on balls getting past the catcher.)

DRA is set to the scale of runs allowed per nine innings (RA9) instead of ERA, which makes DRA's scale slightly higher than ERA's. Because of this, for ease of use, we're supplying DRA-, which is much easier for the reader to parse. As with DRC+, DRA- is an "index" stat, meaning instead of using some arbitrary and shifting number to denote what's "good," average is always 100. The reason that it uses a minus rather than a plus is because like ERA, a lower number is better. Therefore a 75 DRA- describes a performance 25 percent better than average, whereas a 150 DRA- means that either a pitcher is getting extremely lucky with their results, or getting ready to try a new pitch.

Since the last time you picked up an edition of this book, we've also made a few minor changes to DRA to make it better. Recent research into "tunneling"—the act of throwing consecutive pitches that appear similar from a batter's point of view until after the swing decision point–data has given us a new contextual factor to account for in DRA: plate distance. This refers to the distance between successive pitches as they approach the plate, and while it has a smaller effect than factors like velocity or whiff rate, it still can help explain pitcher strikeout rate in our model.

Recently Added Descriptive Statistics

Returning to our 2021 edition of the book are a few figures which recently appeared. These numbers may be a little bit more familiar to those of you who have spent some time investigating baseball statistics.

Fastball Percentage

Our fastball percentage (FA%) statistic measures how frequently a pitcher throws a pitch classified as a "fastball," measured as a percentage of overall pitches thrown. We qualify three types of fastballs:

1. The traditional four-seam fastball;
2. The two-seam fastball or sinker;
3. "Hard cutters," which are pitches that have the movement profile of a cut fastball and are used as the pitcher's primary offering or in place of a more traditional fastball.

For example, a pitcher with a FA% of 67 throws any combination of these three pitches about two-thirds of the time.

Whiff Rate

Everybody loves a swing and a miss, and whiff rate (Whiff%) measures how frequently pitchers induce a swinging strike. To calculate Whiff%, we add up all the pitches thrown that ended with a swinging strike, then divide that number by a pitcher's total pitches thrown. Most often, high whiff rates correlate with high strikeout rates (and overall effective pitcher performance).

Called Strike Probability

Called Strike Probability (CSP) is a number that represents the likelihood that all of a pitcher's pitches will be called a strike while controlling for location, pitcher and batter handedness, umpire and count. Here's how it works: on each pitch, our model determines how many times (out of 100) that a similar pitch was called for a strike given those factors mentioned above, and when normalized for each batter's strike zone. Then we average the CSP for all pitches thrown by a pitcher in a season, and that gives us the yearly CSP percentage you see in the stats boxes.

As you might imagine, pitchers with a higher CSP are more likely to work in the zone, where pitchers with a lower CSP are likely locating their pitches outside the normal strike zone, for better or for worse.

Projections

Many of you aren't turning to this book just for a look at what a player has done, but for a look at what a player is going to do: the PECOTA projections. PECOTA, initially developed by Nate Silver (who has moved on to greater fame as a political analyst), consists of three parts:

1. Major-league equivalencies, which use minor-league statistics to project how a player will perform in the major leagues;
2. Baseline forecasts, which use weighted averages and regression to the mean to estimate a player's current true talent level; and
3. Aging curves, which uses the career paths of comparable players to estimate how a player's statistics are likely to change over time.

With all those important things covered, let's take a look at what's in the book this year.

Team Prospectus

Most of this book is composed of team chapters, with one for each of the 30 major-league franchises. On the first page of each chapter, you'll see a box that contains some of the key statistics for each team as well as a very inviting stadium diagram.

We start with the team name, their unadjusted 2020 win-loss record, and their divisional ranking. Beneath that are a host of other team statistics. **Pythag** presents an adjusted 2020 winning percentage, calculated by taking runs scored per game (**RS/G**) and runs allowed per game (**RA/G**) for the team, and running them through a version of Bill James' Pythagorean formula that was refined and improved by David Smyth and Brandon Heipp. (The formula is called "Pythagenpat," which is equally fun to type and to say.)

Next up is **DRC+**, described earlier, to indicate the overall hitting ability of the team either above or below league-average. Run prevention on the pitching side is covered by **DRA** (also mentioned earlier) and another metric: Fielding Independent Pitching (**FIP**), which calculates another ERA-like statistic based on strikeouts, walks, and home runs recorded. Defensive Efficiency Rating (**DER**) tells us the percentage of balls in play turned into outs for the team, and is a quick fielding shorthand that rounds out run prevention.

After that, we have several measures related to roster composition, as opposed to on-field performance. **B-Age** and **P-Age** tell us the average age of a team's batters and pitchers, respectively. **Payroll** is the combined team payroll for all on-field players, and Doug Pappas' Marginal Dollars per Marginal Win (**M$/MW**) tells us how much money a team spent to earn production above replacement level.

Next to each of these stats, we've listed each team's MLB rank in that category from first to 30th. In this, first always indicates a positive outcome and 30th a negative outcome, except in the case of salary—first is highest.

After the franchise statistics, we share a few items about the team's home ballpark. There's the aforementioned diagram of the park's dimensions (including distances to the outfield wall), a graphic showing the height of the wall from the left-field pole to the right-field pole, and a table showing three-year park factors for the stadium. The park factors are displayed as indexes where 100 is average, 110 means that the park inflates the statistic in question by 10 percent, and 90 means that the park deflates the statistic in question by 10 percent.

On the second page of each team chapter, you'll find three graphs. The first is **Payroll History** and helps you see how the team's payroll has compared to the MLB and divisional average payrolls over time. Payroll figures are current as of January 1, 2021; with so many free agents still unsigned as of this writing, the final 2021 figure will likely be significantly different for many teams. (In the meantime, you can always find the most current data at Baseball Prospectus' Cot's Baseball Contracts page.)

The second graph is **Future Commitments** and helps you see the team's future outlays, if any.

The third graph is **Farm System Ranking** and displays how the Baseball Prospectus prospect team has ranked the organization's farm system since 2007.

After the graphs, we have a **Personnel** section that lists many of the important decision-makers and upper-level field and operations staff members for the franchise, as well as any former Baseball Prospectus staff members who are currently part of the organization. (In very rare circumstances, someone might be on both lists!)

Position Players

After all that information and a thoughtful bylined essay covering each team, we present our player comments. These are also bylined, but due to frequent franchise shifts during the offseason, our bylines are more a rough guide than a perfect accounting of who wrote what.

Each player is listed with the major-league team that employed him as of early January 2021. If a player changed teams after that point via free agency, trade, or any other method, you'll be able to find them in the chapter for their previous squad.

As an example, take a look at the player comment for Padres shortstop Fernando Tatis Jr.: the stat block that accompanies his written comment is at the top of this page. First we cover biographical information (age is as of June 30, 2021) before moving onto the stats themselves. Our statistic columns include standard identifying information like **YEAR**, **TEAM**, **LVL** (level of affiliated play) and **AGE** before getting into the numbers. Next, we provide raw, untranslated

www.baseballprospectus.com

Fernando Tatis Jr. SS
Born: 01/02/99   Age: 22   Bats: R   Throws: R
Height: 6'3"   Weight: 217   Origin: International Free Agent, 2015

YEAR	TEAM	LVL	AGE	PA	R	2B	3B	HR	RBI	BB	K	SB	CS	AVG/OBP/SLG
2018	SA	AA	19	394	77	22	4	16	43	33	109	16	5	.286/.355/.507
2019	SD	MLB	20	372	61	13	6	22	53	30	110	16	6	.317/.379/.590
2020	SD	MLB	21	257	50	11	2	17	45	27	61	11	3	.277/.366/.571
2021 FS	SD	MLB	22	600	95	24	4	31	81	50	165	17	8	.263/.331/.499
2021 DC	SD	MLB	22	628	100	25	4	32	85	53	173	19	8	.263/.331/.499

Comparables: Darryl Strawberry, Bo Bichette, Ronald Acuña Jr.

YEAR	TEAM	LVL	AGE	PA	DRC+	BABIP	BRR	FRAA	WARP
2018	SA	AA	19	394	136	.370	3.0	SS(83): -1.9	2.4
2019	SD	MLB	20	372	118	.410	7.1	SS(83): 0.9	3.4
2020	SD	MLB	21	257	126	.306	0.7	SS(57): -5.5	0.9
2021 FS	SD	MLB	22	600	126	.318	1.7	SS -1	3.9
2021 DC	SD	MLB	22	628	126	.318	1.8	SS -1	4.0

numbers like you might find on the back of your dad's baseball cards: **PA** (plate appearances), **R** (runs), **2B** (doubles), **3B** (triples), **HR** (home runs), **RBI** (runs batted in), **BB** (walks), **K** (strikeouts), **SB** (stolen bases) and **CS** (caught stealing).

Following the basic stats is **Whiff%** (whiff rate), which denotes how often, when a batter swings, he fails to make contact with the ball. Another way to think of this number is an inverse of a hitter's contact rate.

Next, we have unadjusted "slash" statistics: **AVG** (batting average), **OBP** (on-base percentage) and **SLG** (slugging percentage). Following the slash line is **DRC+** (Deserved Runs Created Plus), which we described earlier as total offensive expected contribution compared to the league average.

BABIP (batting average on balls in play) tells us how often a ball in play fell for a hit, and can help us identify whether a batter may have been lucky or not ... but note that high BABIPs also tend to follow the great hitters of our time, as well as speedy singles hitters who put the ball on the ground.

The next item is **BRR** (Baserunning Runs), which covers all of a player's baserunning accomplishments including (but not limited to) swiped bags and failed attempts. Next is **FRAA** (Fielding Runs Above Average), which also includes the number of games previously played at each position noted in parentheses. Multi-position players have only their two most frequent positions listed here, but their total FRAA number reflects all positions played.

Our last column here is **WARP** (Wins Above Replacement Player). WARP estimates the total value of a player, which means for hitters it takes into account hitting runs above average (calculated using the DRC+ model), BRR and FRAA. Then, it makes an adjustment for positions played and gives the player a credit for plate appearances based upon the difference between "replacement level"—which is derived from the quality of players added to a team's roster after the start of the season–and the league average.

The final line just below the stats box is **PECOTA** data, which is discussed further in a following section.

Catchers

Catchers are a special breed, and thus they have earned their own separate box which displays some of the defensive metrics that we've built just for them. As an example, let's check out Yasmani Grandal.

YEAR	TEAM	P. COUNT	FRM RUNS	BLK RUNS	THRW RUNS	TOT RUNS
2018	LAD	16816	15.7	0.8	0.1	16.5
2019	MIL	18740	19.4	1.8	-0.1	21.1
2020	CHW	4830	3.7	0.3	-0.2	3.8
2021	CHW	14430	16.7	-0.6	1.0	17.1
2021	CHW	14430	16.7	0.4	1.0	18.0

The **YEAR** and **TEAM** columns match what you'd find in the other stat box. **P. COUNT** indicates the number of pitches thrown while the catcher was behind the plate, including swinging strikes, fouls and balls in play. **FRM RUNS** is the total run value the catcher provided (or cost) his team by influencing the umpire to call strikes where other catchers did not. **BLK RUNS** expresses the total run value above or below average for the catcher's ability to prevent wild pitches and passed balls. **THRW RUNS** is calculated using a similar model as the previous two statistics, and it measures a catcher's ability to throw out basestealers but also to dissuade them from testing his arm in the first place. It takes into account factors like the pitcher (including his delivery and pickoff move) and baserunner (who could be as fast as Billy Hamilton or as slow as Yonder Alonso). **TOT RUNS** is the sum of all of the previous three statistics.

Pitchers

Let's give our pitchers a turn, using 2020 AL Cy Young winner Shane Bieber as our example. Take a look at his stat block: the first line and the **YEAR**, **TEAM**, **LVL** and **AGE** columns are the same as in the position player example earlier.

Here too, we have a series of columns that display raw, unadjusted statistics compiled by the pitcher over the course of a season: **W** (wins), **L** (losses), **SV** (saves), **G** (games pitched), **GS** (games started), **IP** (innings pitched), **H** (hits allowed) and **HR** (home runs allowed). Next we have two statistics that are rates: **BB/9** (walks per nine innings) and **K/9** (strikeouts per nine innings), before returning to the unadjusted K (strikeouts).

www.baseballprospectus.com

Next up is **GB%** (ground ball percentage), which is the percentage of all batted balls that were hit on the ground, including both outs and hits. Remember, this is based on observational data and subject to human error, so please approach this with a healthy dose of skepticism.

BABIP (batting average on balls in play) is calculated using the same methodology as it is for position players, but it often tells us more about a pitcher than it does a hitter. With pitchers, a high BABIP is often due to poor defense or bad luck, and can often be an indicator of potential rebound, and a low BABIP may be cause to expect performance regression. (A typical league-average BABIP is close to .290-.300.)

The metrics **WHIP** (walks plus hits per inning pitched) and **ERA** (earned run average) are old standbys: WHIP measures walks and hits allowed on a per-inning basis, while ERA measures earned runs on a nine-inning basis. Neither of these stats are translated or adjusted.

DRA- (Deserved Run Average) was described at length earlier, and measures how the pitcher "deserved" to perform compared to other pitchers. Please note that since we lack all the data points that would make for a "real" DRA for minor-league events, the DRA- displayed for minor league partial-seasons is based off of different data. (That data is a modified version of our cFIP metric, which you can find more information about on our website.)

Shane Bieber   RHP
Born: 05/31/95   Age: 26   Bats: R   Throws: R
Height: 6'3"   Weight: 200   Origin: Round 4, 2016 Draft (#122 overall)

YEAR	TEAM	LVL	AGE	W	L	SV	G	GS	IP	H	HR	BB/9	K/9	K	GB%	BABIP
2018	AKR	AA	23	3	0	0	5	5	31	26	1	0.3	8.7	30	47.3%	.278
2018	COL	AAA	23	3	1	0	8	8	48^2	30	3	1.1	8.7	47	52.0%	.227
2018	CLE	MLB	23	11	5	0	20	19	114^2	130	13	1.8	9.3	118	46.2%	.356
2019	CLE	MLB	24	15	8	0	34	33	214^1	186	31	1.7	10.9	259	44.4%	.298
2020	CLE	MLB	25	8	1	0	12	12	77^1	46	7	2.4	14.2	122	48.4%	.267
2021 FS	CLE	MLB	26	10	6	0	26	26	150	121	18	2.1	11.7	195	45.5%	.297
2021 DC	CLE	MLB	26	14	7	0	30	30	196.7	159	24	2.1	11.7	257	45.5%	.297

Comparables: Luis Severino, Danny Salazar, Joe Musgrove

YEAR	TEAM	LVL	AGE	WHIP	ERA	DRA-	WARP	MPH	FB%	WHF	CSP
2018	AKR	AA	23	0.87	1.16	61	0.9				
2018	COL	AAA	23	0.74	1.66	69	1.2				
2018	CLE	MLB	23	1.33	4.55	74	2.6	94.7	57.4%	26.2%	
2019	CLE	MLB	24	1.05	3.28	75	4.9	94.4	45.8%	30.8%	
2020	CLE	MLB	25	0.87	1.63	53	2.6	95.3	53.6%	40.7%	
2021 FS	CLE	MLB	26	1.04	2.44	64	4.4	94.7	50.0%	33.2%	44.2%
2021 DC	CLE	MLB	26	1.04	2.44	64	5.8	94.7	50.0%	33.2%	44.2%

Just like with hitters, **WARP** (Wins Above Replacement Player) is a total value metric that puts pitchers of all stripes on the same scale as position players. We use DRA as the primary input for our calculation of WARP. You might notice that relief pitchers (due to their limited innings) may have a lower WARP than you were expecting or than you might see in other WARP-like metrics. WARP does not take leverage into account, just the actions a pitcher performs and the expected value of those actions ... which ends up judging high-leverage relief pitchers differently than you might imagine given their prestige and market value.

MPH gives you the pitcher's 95th percentile velocity for the noted season, in order to give you an idea of what the *peak* fastball velocity a pitcher possesses. Since this comes from our pitch-tracking data, it is not publicly available for minor-league pitchers.

Finally, we display the three new pitching metrics we described earlier. **FB%** (fastball percentage) gives you the percentage of fastballs thrown out of all pitches. **WHF** (whiff rate) tells you the percentage of swinging strikes induced out of all pitches. **CSP** (called strike probability) expresses the likelihood of all pitches thrown to result in a called strike, after controlling for factors like handedness, umpire, pitch type, count and location.

PECOTA

All players have PECOTA projections for 2021, as well as a set of other numbers that describe the performance of comparable players according to PECOTA. All projections for 2021 are for the player at the date we went to press in early January and are projected into the league and park context as indicated by the team abbreviation. (Note that players at very low levels of the minors are too unpredictable to assess using these numbers.) All PECOTA projected statistics represent a player's projected major-league performance.

How we're doing that is a little different this season. There are really two different values that go into the final stat line that you see for PECOTA: How a player performs, and how much playing time he'll be given to perform it. In the past we've estimated playing time based on each team's roster and depth charts, and we'll continue to do that. These projections are denoted as **2021 DC**.

But in many cases, a player won't be projected for major-league playing time; most of the time this is because they aren't projected to be major-league players at all, but still developing as prospects. Or perhaps a player will provide Triple-A depth, only to have an opportunity open up because of injury. For these purposes, we're also supplying a second projection, labeled **2021 FS**, or full season. This is what we would project the player to provide in 600 plate appearances or 150 innings pitched.

Below the projections are the player's three highest-scoring comparable players as determined by PECOTA. All comparables represent a snapshot of how the listed player was performing at the same age as the current player, so if a

23-year-old pitcher is compared to Bartolo Colón, he's actually being compared to a 23-year-old Colón, not the version that pitched for the Rangers in 2018, nor to Colón's career as a whole.

A few points about pitcher projections. First, we aren't yet projecting peak velocity, so that column will be blank in the PECOTA lines. Second, projecting DRA is trickier than evaluating past performance, because it is unclear how deserving each pitcher will be of his anticipated outcomes. However, we know that another DRA-related statistic–contextual FIP or cFIP-estimates future run scoring very well. So for PECOTA, the projected DRA- figures you see are based on the past cFIPs generated by the pitcher and comparable players over time, along with the other factors described above.

If you're familiar with PECOTA, then you'll have noticed that the projection system often appears bullish on players coming off a bad year and bearish on players coming off a good year. (This is because the system weights several previous seasons, not just the most recent one.) In addition, we publish the 50th percentile projections for each player–which is smack in the middle of the range of projected production—which tends to mean PECOTA stat lines don't often have extreme results like 40 home runs or 250 strikeouts in a given season. In essence, PECOTA doesn't project very many extreme seasons.

Managers

After all those wonderful team chapters, we've got statistics for each big-league manager, all of whom are organized by alphabetical order. Here you'll find a block including an extraordinary amount of information collected from each manager's entire career. For more information on the acronyms and what they mean, please visit the Glossary at www.baseballprospectus.com.

There is one important metric that we'd like to call attention to, and you'll find it next to each manager's name: **wRM+** (weighted reliever management plus). Developed by Rob Arthur and Rian Watt, wRM+ investigates how good a manager is at using their best relievers during the moments of highest leverage, using both our proprietary DRA metric as well as Leverage Index. wRM+ is scaled to a league average of 100, and a wRM+ of 105 indicates that relievers were used approximately five percent "better" than average. On the other hand, a wRM+ of 95 would tell us the team used its relievers five percent "worse" than the average team.

While wRM+ does not have an extremely strong correlation with a manager, it is statistically significant; this means that a manager is not *entirely* responsible for a team's wRM+, but does have some effect on that number.

Part 1: Team Analysis

Performance Graphs

Payroll History (in millions)

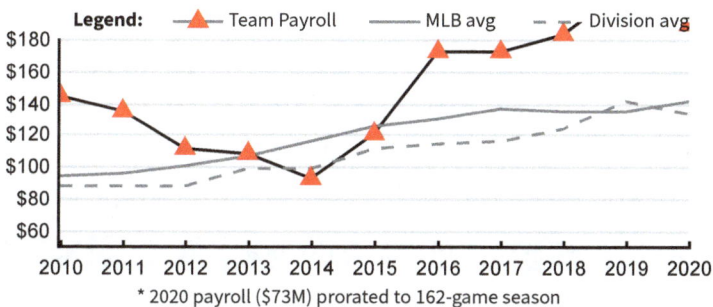

*2020 payroll ($73M) prorated to 162-game season

Future Commitments (in millions)

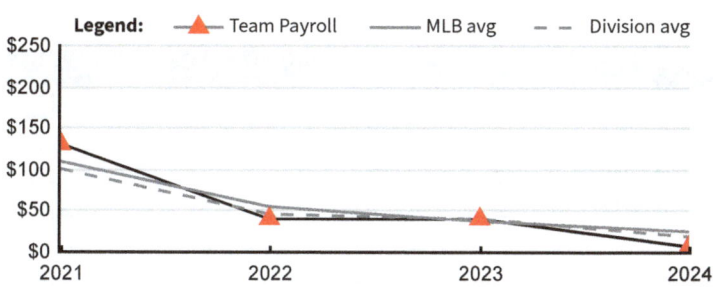

Farm System Ranking

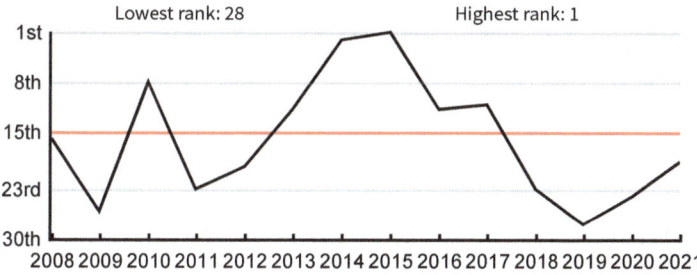

2020 Team Performance

ACTUAL STANDINGS

Team	W	L	Pct
CHC	**34**	**26**	**0.567**
CIN	31	29	0.517
STL	30	28	0.517
MIL	29	31	0.483
PIT	19	41	0.317

dWIN% STANDINGS

Team	W	L	Pct
CIN	32	28	0.537
MIL	29	31	0.496
CHC	**27**	**33**	**0.465**
STL	26	34	0.436
PIT	20	40	0.344

TOP HITTERS

Player	WARP
Jason Heyward	1.5
Willson Contreras	1.1
Javier Báez	0.9

TOP PITCHERS

Player	WARP
Yu Darvish	2.0
Kyle Hendricks	1.3
Ryan Tepera	0.4

VITAL STATISTICS

Statistic Name	Value	Rank
Pythagenpat	.546	10th
dWin%	.465	16th
Runs Scored per Game	4.42	20th
Runs Allowed per Game	4.00	7th
Deserved Runs Created Plus	97	18th
Deserved Run Average Minus	93	10th
Fielding Independent Pitching	4.19	9th
Defensive Efficiency Rating	.711	5th
Batter Age	28.4	17th
Pitcher Age	31.0	29th
Payroll	$73.0M	6th
Marginal $ per Marginal Win	$3.5M	15th

2021 Team Projections

PROJECTED STANDINGS

Team	W	L	Pct	+/-
MIL	89.1	72.9	0.550	10
Adding Kolten Wong doesn't quite make this an above-average lineup, but it improves their run prevention. Playoff hopes hinge on Christian Yelich being himself again.				
CHC	84.9	77.1	0.524	-6
Change, though painful, will give them an overdue chance to evaluate new options.				
STL	80.4	81.6	0.496	0
Nolan Arenado makes them favorites in the NL Central, but real parity with the goliaths on the coasts is still a ways off.				
CIN	79.3	82.7	0.490	-4
Traded or non-tendered several key role players to save money, and their Cy Young winner left as a free agent.				
PIT	59.5	102.5	0.367	8
This year will be about sorting out shortstop, hoping for progress from Mitch Keller, and enjoying Ke'Bryan Hayes--but not much more.				

TOP PROJECTED HITTERS

Player	WARP
Anthony Rizzo	3.9
Willson Contreras	3.2
Kris Bryant	2.9

TOP PROJECTED PITCHERS

Player	WARP
Kyle Hendricks	3.3
Zach Davies	1.8
Alec Mills	1.7

FARM SYSTEM REPORT

Top Prospect	Number of Top 101 Prospects
Brailyn Marquez, #63	4

KEY DEDUCTIONS

Player	WARP
Yu Darvish	3.9
Kyle Schwarber	3.0
José Quintana	1.9
Jon Lester	1.0
Victor Caratini	0.4
Albert Almora Jr.	0.3
José Martínez	0.3

KEY ADDITIONS

Player	WARP
Joc Pederson	2.5
Zach Davies	1.8
Trevor Williams	1.1
Jonathan Holder	0.4

Team Personnel

President, BasebalL Operations
Jed Hoyer

Assistant General Manager
Randy Bush

Assistant General Manager
Jeff Greenberg

Senior Vice President, Player Personnel
Jason McLeod

Manager
David Ross

BP Alumni
Bryan Cole
Jeremy Greenhouse

Wrigley Field Stats

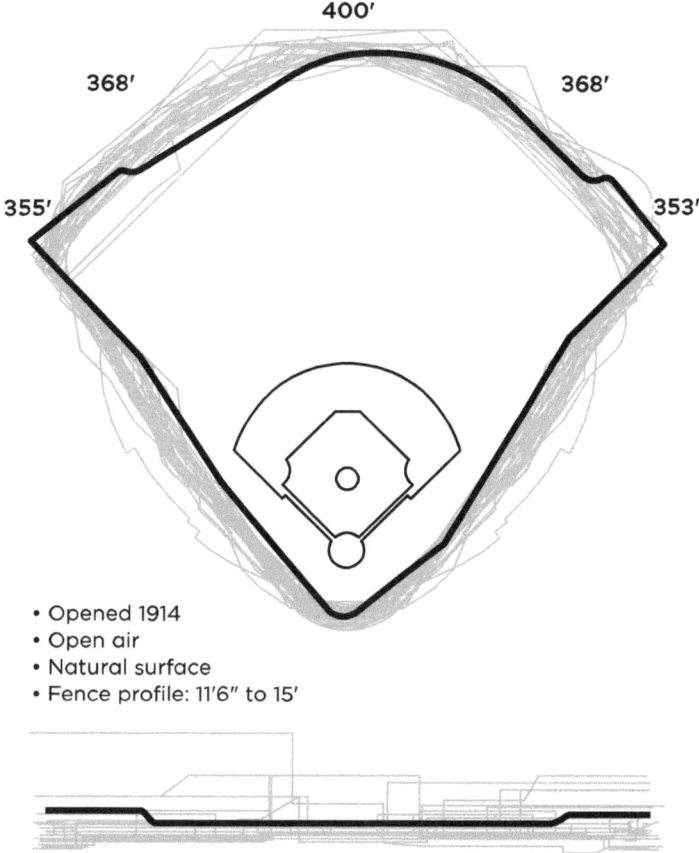

- Opened 1914
- Open air
- Natural surface
- Fence profile: 11'6" to 15'

Three-Year Park Factors

Runs	Runs/RH	Runs/LH	HR/RH	HR/LH
103	104	100	104	94

Cubs Team Analysis

My husband and I started dating on August 15, 2016. The Cubs were 73-43 at the time, and it was a scheduled off day, which I told him was the only reason that we were able to go out that evening. I joked with friends the next morning, saying that if he made it through not only a Cubs postseason run, but also the 2016 election *and* the debut of *Pitch* (a show about the first woman to pitch in MLB that seemed to have been made specifically for me, and me alone), there was no way we *weren't* getting married. The next day the Cubs won a 4-0 game against the Cardinals and went on to finish August as their best month, with a 22-6 record; we were off to the races.

Being a Cubs fan from 2007-16 was a privilege. I wasn't new, and I had always been proud, but these were the first years as a lifelong in which I was *confident*. Even before Theo Epstein and Joe Maddon came aboard, down in the dugout Lou Pinella brought with him an (often delightfully aggressive) winning energy to the clubhouse. "Sweet" Lou would go to the mats for his players, to the point of ejection and even a four-day suspension. He believed in that team, and through his outbursts early in the 2007 season, we fans could at least tell that Pinella could *see* the same problems we did. What's more, he was willing to make adjustments to fix them, and so, while we ended up swept in the first round of playoffs that year, it felt like there was a hint of promise.

It's possible that I remember those years fondly—even the stretch of iffy seasons from 2010-12—because I remember the world of that era fondly as well. There was a recession, multiple endless wars, a few small-scale pandemics and also the Kardashians, but I was in my early 20s, a fresh college graduate with a job. I had a New York City apartment. Barack Obama was president. *Mad Men* kept getting *better*! The world was my oyster, and when Chicago hired Theo Epstein to be the team's president in 2011, it felt like my team had it made too. Sure, we were both going to have to lose for a little while (Theo made that clear, and so did the paychecks from my job at an education non-profit) but we also both had *plans*, and our timelines aligned. We were going to build our success together.

And the weird thing is … we did. 2016 was one of the best years of my personal and professional life, a culmination of hard work that began in 2011 (mixed with a bit of good luck, just like in any baseball victory) and the giddiness of being in a new relationship. Cynics like to say that your team winning a big game doesn't really affect *you* personally, but after we won the World Series that year, the single, joyous memory of a glass beer stein exploding against a wall just inches above my head at a Cubs bar in New York City erupted after that final out is the sole thing that kept me functioning after the results of the 2016 election came in a week later.

Needless to say that with another contentious election approaching, I—a supremely superstitious baseball fan getting excited for spring training while also watching a pandemic creep across the globe—did not want the Cubs to win the World Series in 2020.

I *did* want to watch at least 100 games, though. Much like in 2016, I was kind of counting on baseball to be the *thing* that got me through another year in a world filled with massive, external challenges that I had no way of controlling. With accomplished, World Series-winning players like Anthony Rizzo, Kris Bryant, Kyle Hendricks and Willson Conteras playing under the management of former teammate David Ross, I expected a lively and promising year, like the ones we'd had in '17 and '18—a season that wouldn't end signaling the need to rebuild, but maybe just to retool. Perhaps we would need to fill out the bench, tighten up our bats or secure a second shortstop so that a Baez injury didn't cause an existential crisis.

Things played out differently, but once again in a year that was shaping up to be yet a professional and personal gem akin to 2016 (maybe *I'm* the problem?), I was determined to make the best of it. A 60-game season starting in July? That was just more time for players to get in shape and better weather to play in. No fans in the stand? Fewer distractions. Weird game start times? I told myself that the sun and shadows at Wrigley wouldn't be able to play their usual tricks with outfielders. Universal Designated Hitter in the National League? Well, I also didn't like Brussels sprouts until age 31, so maybe it was time to give the DH a fresh opportunity to win me over too. Weirder things had already happened in 2020, after all.

The season looked nothing like anything we'd seen in baseball's living memory. The world at large was so off-kilter that judging any player or team on their 2020 performances seems almost unfair. (Sorry, Dodgers fans.) It was a funhouse mirror of a year, where Kyle Schwarber, of all people, ended the year as the worst batter in the National League. The Cubs still managed to piece together wins, opening the season with a Hendricks shutout and paving the way for several near-misses by Jon Lester, Alec Mills and then Hendricks again. Cubs fans saw the first no-hitter (by Mills) since Jake Arrieta's '16 gem. They even made the (modified) playoffs.

In this mirrorverse of a year, Jason Heyward was also having one of his best seasons as Cub—something I've wanted for him since he used part of his initial salary to pay travel, room, and board for David Ross' wife and three kids for away games during his first season in town in 2016. His status as a fundamentally good human being who shows leadership on the field and in the clubhouse (during 17-minute rain delays and otherwise) makes him deeply easy to root for.

Yet that same fundamental goodness was also the final straw in my 2020 season. Heyward, the clear season MVP, pulled double-duty serving as both an offensive and a moral leader for the Cubs. He would've appeared in 51, not 50 games had he (and other players around the league) not made the choice to sit out on August 26 in protest after Jacob Blake was shot and paralyzed by police in Kenosha, Wisconsin. It's said that his teammates didn't want to leave Heyward out on the limb of protest alone, and that they offered to sit out with him. He told them, "No, go play the game. I don't think the game should be canceled. But I think I have to do what I have to do."

This is the part where I tell you that I am a Black woman; that I believe Jason Heyward did the right thing in sitting out; and that as someone who is used to being alone in a room, adrift in opinion, and put on the spot due to my race and gender, I am still in this offseason wrestling with how I feel about the Cubs' decision to play that day instead of rallying behind their Black teammate like six other teams did. A teammate who had been there for them countless times, Heyward literally shepherded them through a king-making season, helped them earn a ring (and a third Gold Glove for himself in the process) and proved his worth again and again. As my feelings about baseball so often do mirror and reflect how I feel about the world and the ways in which I inhabit it, I suspect I will continue to think and look back at that game in the same way I replay personal experiences involving those complicated topics of race, protest and social justice over and over again in my head. I'm not angry at any specific person, or even the team as a whole; the situation just ... well, it didn't feel great.

Beyond anything else that happened in 2020, that August 26 game is the main reason I do not anticipate looking back at this season with the fondness or good humor that I occasionally look back at those that fared worse for my Cubs. Watching baseball (or any team sport aside from basketball in the Disney bubble, really) last year was already a moral quandary, and eventually it began to feel actively *bad*. It felt (and, frankly, probably *was*) like something that should not be happening. Like we had not earned it as a country. As my anxiety about the impending election ramped up I became actively worried when we made the playoffs again, and frankly, I was perfectly fine when we were swept, as is our way, this time by the Marlins. (Another strange twist, part of this terrible year that I finally could put to rest.) Baseball was no longer a refuge and I couldn't take the Cubs' struggle on as my own, as I once had, because they had *literally* chosen not to take mine on in return. Like a parent, I wasn't mad, but I was disappointed.

When Theo Epstein announced that he was resigning from his position, I was surprised at my own ambivalence. Then came the offseason and the trade rumors, with names that should have been terrifying, like Anthony Rizzo and

Chicago Cubs 2021

Kris Bryant. It became clear that the core of the team Epstein had planned so carefully for in his rebuilding years might no longer exist. In fact, Heyward's name was one of the few that *wasn't* being batted around as a potential trade, likely because he has $65 million coming his way over the next three years. We can be fairly certain that he'll remain a Cub in 2021 and beyond, serving as the Cubs' Alex Gordon.

Plenty of teams are saddled with bad contracts. What makes Heyward's deal easier to stomach is that it comes with a good person—one who played a role in a championship; one who has demonstrated leadership ability; and one who can assist in the transition from this core to the next by imparting his wisdom on his younger teammates.

For all the good Heyward could do in a statesman role, we have to acknowledge that he won't be around forever. His eight-year contract leaves him eligible for free agency approaching in '23 might look far off, but if 2020 has shown us anything it's that April is approximately 76 days long, not 30, and that a year can last anywhere between four and 99 months. Along with newly promoted president Jed Hoyer and whoever will take on Hoyer's former role as GM, Ross and the Cubs need to be looking back at their farm system and (with all the patience and sacrifice necessary) returning it to Epstein-like shape. The focus cannot simply be on 2021, but the next several years, too.

After wanting to see it continue forever in spring, I see a lot of rebuilding in this team's future, and I think that is *good*. Given how deeply superstition and a keen attention to signs (from the catcher, yes, but also the universe) run through baseball, but especially Cubs fandom, 2021 feels like a particularly apt time for this process to commence. America will officially enter its own "rebuilding" period, albeit a bit late. It wasn't leadership that was necessarily my first choice, but it is leadership that I know will set the ship right in order to get us to a point where we can start getting some of those big wins again. It'll be a lot easier to afford playoff tickets after our student loan debt is cancelled, eh? *This* is the sort of mirror I appreciate baseball holding up to my life.

Though 2020 may not have been the season Cubs fans wanted, it wasn't quite the year we wanted either. Whether it's moving back to or from the places we used to call home, finally having the opportunity to reconnect with friends and family in person, picking up the pieces of an major life event lost to the chaos of 2020 or simply reacclimating to living largely outside the confines of our homes, the next 18 to 24 months are going to be a rebuilding time for nearly all of us—on and off the baseball diamond. We're gonna have to lose a little, again, in order to right the ship and eventually win big, but we're gonna be doing it *together*.

—Kendra James is a freelance pop culture writer and critic.

Part 2: Player Analysis

Chicago Cubs 2021

PLAYER COMMENTS WITH GRAPHS

Javier Báez SS
Born: 12/01/92   Age: 28   Bats: R   Throws: R
Height: 6'0"   Weight: 190   Origin: Round 1, 2011 Draft (#9 overall)

YEAR	TEAM	LVL	AGE	PA	R	2B	3B	HR	RBI	BB	K	SB	CS	AVG/OBP/SLG
2018	CHC	MLB	25	645	101	40	9	34	111	29	167	21	9	.290/.326/.554
2019	CHC	MLB	26	561	89	38	4	29	85	28	156	11	7	.281/.316/.531
2020	CHC	MLB	27	235	27	9	1	8	24	7	75	3	0	.203/.238/.360
2021 FS	CHC	MLB	28	600	80	27	3	28	91	30	185	12	6	.246/.294/.456
2021 DC	CHC	MLB	28	625	83	29	3	29	95	31	193	13	6	.246/.294/.456

Comparables: Tim Anderson, Chris Taylor, Jhonny Peralta

Is the most exciting player in baseball still the most exciting player in baseball if no fans are allowed in attendance? In 2020, that answer was in the negative. "I get motivated from my fans," Báez said. "It's really weird, to be honest. It's not an excuse because it's the same for every team. But everybody's different. Some of them like 'em, some of them don't like having fans. We have to deal with it." How much the fan-less experience really affected Báez's play is impossible to judge, but what's not is that the former MVP candidate suffered through the worst season of his career, flailing away at a rate worse than we've ever seen from the already swing-happy shortstop. Báez doesn't need to be patient and in control of the strike zone to be successful, he proved as much the last few years. He does, apparently, need cheering (or booing) fans. If that's the case, 2021 will be as important as ever, as it's the final year before Báez reaches free agency—and, as of press time, it seemed doubtful that fans will be there to start the season.

YEAR	TEAM	LVL	AGE	PA	DRC+	BABIP	BRR	FRAA	WARP
2018	CHC	MLB	25	645	119	.347	3.2	2B(104): -0.6, SS(65): 1.3, 3B(22): 2.1	4.6
2019	CHC	MLB	26	561	101	.345	4.3	SS(129): 7.2, 3B(1): 0.1	3.9
2020	CHC	MLB	27	235	68	.262	0.5	SS(56): 9.1, LF(1): -0.0	0.9
2021 FS	CHC	MLB	28	600	100	.317	1.0	SS 4, 1B 0	2.3
2021 DC	CHC	MLB	28	625	100	.317	1.1	SS 4	2.5

Javier Báez, continued

Batted Ball Distribution

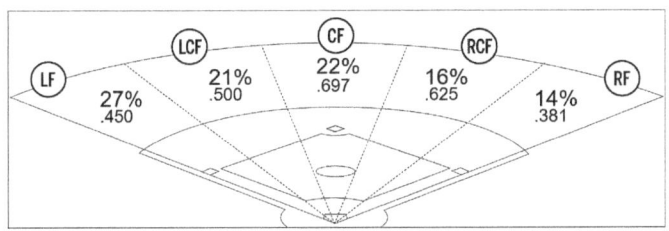

Strike Zone vs LHP Strike Zone vs RHP

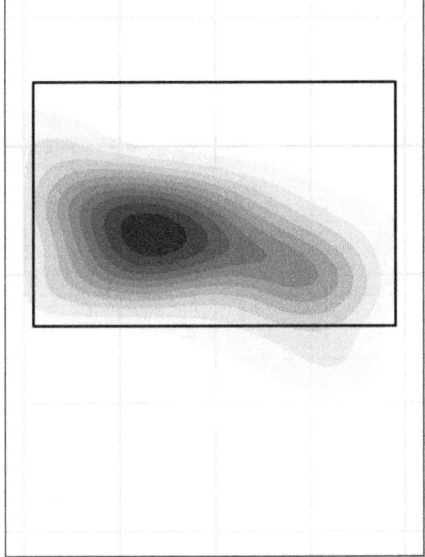

David Bote 3B

Born: 04/07/93   Age: 28   Bats: R   Throws: R
Height: 6'1"   Weight: 205   Origin: Round 18, 2012 Draft (#554 overall)

YEAR	TEAM	LVL	AGE	PA	R	2B	3B	HR	RBI	BB	K	SB	CS	AVG/OBP/SLG
2018	IOW	AAA	25	263	34	10	2	13	41	26	63	3	1	.268/.342/.494
2018	CHC	MLB	25	210	23	9	2	6	33	19	60	3	4	.239/.319/.408
2019	CHC	MLB	26	356	47	17	0	11	41	44	93	5	1	.257/.362/.422
2020	CHC	MLB	27	145	15	3	1	7	29	17	40	2	0	.200/.303/.408
2021 FS	CHC	MLB	28	600	79	25	2	23	78	59	165	2	2	.239/.327/.428
2021 DC	CHC	MLB	28	544	71	23	2	21	71	54	150	2	2	.239/.327/.428

Comparables: Shane Andrews, Andy Tracy, Ian Stewart

Everything about what Bote did for the Cubs in 2020 was pretty much in line with what they saw out of their utility infielder the previous two seasons: plate-discipline numbers, batted-ball data, ball-tracking metrics. If anything, those numbers improved, as Bote started lifting the ball more frequently and hitting the ball harder on average. So, what went wrong? In a word…BABIP. Okay, that's not so much a word as it is a weird acronym, but the point is that Bote got BABIP'd to death in 2020, with that number dropping by more than 100 points from the year prior. That made for a frustrating season, but as Bote sets sail on a new voyage, the prospects of a full, 162-game campaign makes it difficult to worry about him capsizing again.

YEAR	TEAM	LVL	AGE	PA	DRC+	BABIP	BRR	FRAA	WARP
2018	IOW	AAA	25	263	129	.312	-0.2	2B(38): -2.9, SS(15): 1.3, 3B(9): 1.3	1.3
2018	CHC	MLB	25	210	76	.314	-1.0	3B(56): 2.4, 2B(13): -0.6, 1B(2): 0.0	0.2
2019	CHC	MLB	26	356	97	.333	3.7	3B(67): -1.0, 2B(50): 2.0, SS(9): -0.1	1.6
2020	CHC	MLB	27	145	87	.228	0.2	3B(33): -3.2, 2B(7): -0.4, 1B(1): 0.0	-0.3
2021 FS	CHC	MLB	28	600	107	.303	-0.4	3B 0, 2B 0	1.9
2021 DC	CHC	MLB	28	544	107	.303	-0.4	3B 0, 2B 0	1.6

David Bote, continued

Batted Ball Distribution

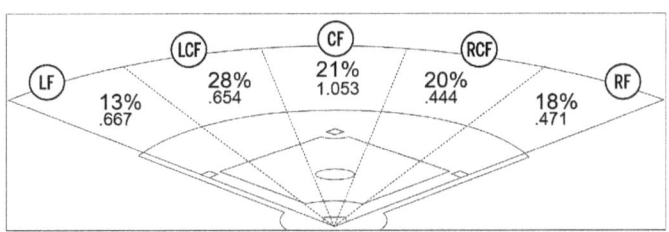

Strike Zone vs LHP   Strike Zone vs RHP

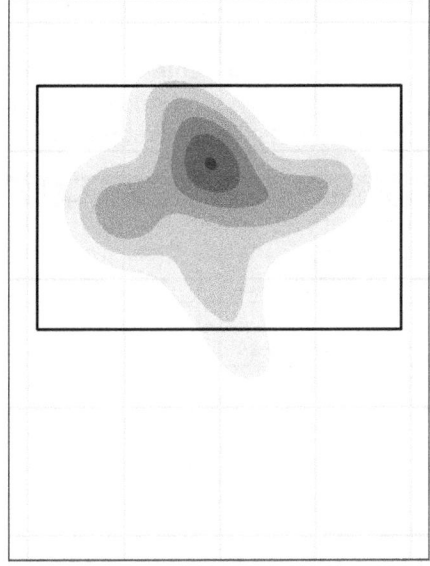

Kris Bryant 3B

Born: 01/04/92 Age: 29 Bats: R Throws: R
Height: 6'5" Weight: 230 Origin: Round 1, 2013 Draft (#2 overall)

YEAR	TEAM	LVL	AGE	PA	R	2B	3B	HR	RBI	BB	K	SB	CS	AVG/OBP/SLG
2018	CHC	MLB	26	457	59	28	3	13	52	48	107	2	4	.272/.374/.460
2019	CHC	MLB	27	634	108	35	1	31	77	74	145	4	0	.282/.382/.521
2020	CHC	MLB	28	147	20	5	1	4	11	12	40	0	0	.206/.293/.351
2021 FS	CHC	MLB	29	600	95	24	2	26	78	71	161	5	3	.244/.355/.457
2021 DC	CHC	MLB	29	654	104	26	2	29	85	77	176	6	3	.244/.355/.457

Comparables: Troy Glaus, Scott Rolen, Evan Longoria

Bryant's year began with news that he had lost his grievance against the Cubs alleging they had manipulated his service time in 2015 in order to gain an extra year of team control. The Cubs did manipulate his service time, of course but Bryant lost the case. He then suffered through a lost year. The list of body parts that betrayed the former MVP included, but was not limited to: oblique, wrist, elbow, finger and back. He also missed time with a gastrointestinal issue. If there's a silver lining in Bryant's year, it's that all the injuries can (and probably should) be blamed for his rotten play. A fully healthy Bryant, it can be reasoned, ought to still be viewed as a cornerstone player at either third base or in an outfield corner. Now entering his walk year, Bryant will have to stay healthy and produce if he wants the kind of contract that led the Cubs to suppress his earning potential in the first place.

YEAR	TEAM	LVL	AGE	PA	DRC+	BABIP	BRR	FRAA	WARP
2018	CHC	MLB	26	457	109	.342	-2.2	3B(86): 0.8, RF(15): -0.0, LF(14): -0.4	1.9
2019	CHC	MLB	27	634	125	.331	2.2	3B(115): -14.3, RF(27): -2.2, LF(23): -1.6	2.7
2020	CHC	MLB	28	147	92	.264	1.4	3B(27): -0.6, LF(4): -0.3, 1B(1): 0.0	0.3
2021 FS	CHC	MLB	29	600	122	.305	-0.2	3B -1, LF 0	2.7
2021 DC	CHC	MLB	29	654	122	.305	-0.3	3B -1, LF 0	2.9

Kris Bryant, continued

Batted Ball Distribution

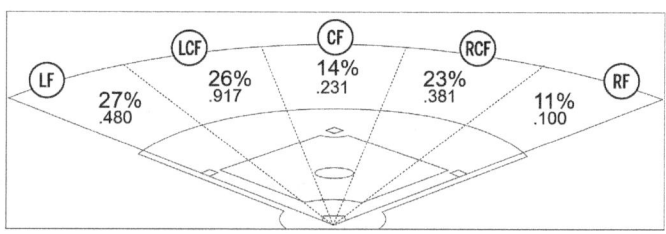

Strike Zone vs LHP   Strike Zone vs RHP

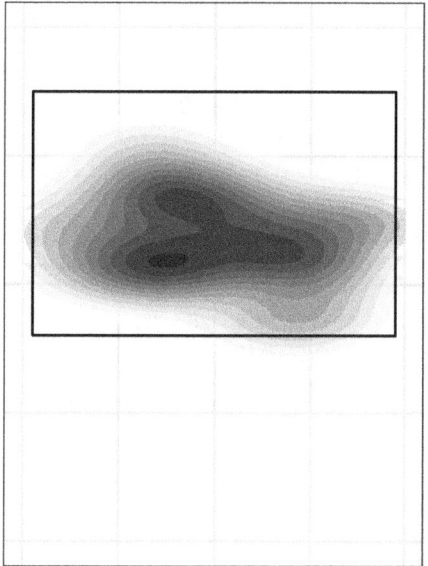

Willson Contreras C

Born: 05/13/92   Age: 29   Bats: R   Throws: R
Height: 6'1"   Weight: 225   Origin: International Free Agent, 2009

YEAR	TEAM	LVL	AGE	PA	R	2B	3B	HR	RBI	BB	K	SB	CS	AVG/OBP/SLG
2018	CHC	MLB	26	544	50	27	5	10	54	53	121	4	1	.249/.339/.390
2019	CHC	MLB	27	409	57	18	2	24	64	38	102	1	2	.272/.355/.533
2020	CHC	MLB	28	225	37	10	0	7	26	20	57	1	2	.243/.356/.407
2021 FS	CHC	MLB	29	600	83	24	2	24	85	60	152	4	3	.251/.349/.447
2021 DC	CHC	MLB	29	511	71	21	2	20	73	51	129	4	2	.251/.349/.447

Comparables: Bobby Estalella, Rick Wilkins, Alex Avila

"But his defense!" was a common retort about Contreras during his three-year ascent into one of the game's best offensive catchers. It wasn't unwarranted, but Contreras—who admitted he hadn't before put much thought into framing—showed marked improvement in his age-28 season. "But his offense!" they'll likely now cry as the commitment to defense coincided with a career-worst batting average and a serious lack of power. Balancing defensive focus with offensive readiness is a challenge for any catcher, but Contreras seems to have found the right equation. Both he and the Cubs should be better for it going forward.

YEAR	TEAM	P. COUNT	FRM RUNS	BLK RUNS	THRW RUNS	TOT RUNS
2018	CHC	18720	-17.8	1.9	0.4	-15.5
2019	CHC	13930	-9.4	0.0	-0.3	-9.7
2020	CHC	5378	2.7	0.4	-0.1	2.9
2021	CHC	15632	-0.8	1.1	0.5	0.8
2021	CHC	15632	-0.8	-0.1	0.5	-0.4

YEAR	TEAM	LVL	AGE	PA	DRC+	BABIP	BRR	FRAA	WARP
2018	CHC	MLB	26	544	90	.313	0.6	C(133): -14.6, LF(5): -0.8, 1B(1): -0.0	0.5
2019	CHC	MLB	27	409	110	.314	-1.9	C(99): -8.7, 1B(2): -0.0, RF(2): 1.1	1.7
2020	CHC	MLB	28	225	108	.307	-0.4	C(41): -0.5	1.1
2021 FS	CHC	MLB	29	600	119	.309	-0.3	C 1, 1B 0	4.0
2021 DC	CHC	MLB	29	511	119	.309	-0.3	C 1	3.2

Willson Contreras, continued

Batted Ball Distribution

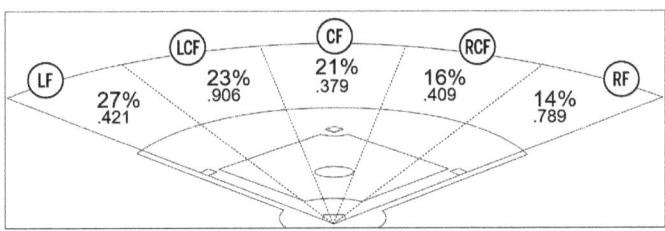

Strike Zone vs LHP   **Strike Zone vs RHP**

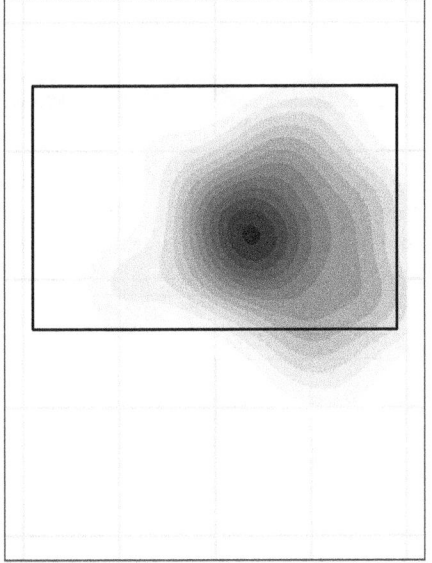

Chicago Cubs 2021

Phillip Ervin RF
Born: 07/15/92 Age: 28 Bats: R Throws: R
Height: 5'10" Weight: 207 Origin: Round 1, 2013 Draft (#27 overall)

YEAR	TEAM	LVL	AGE	PA	R	2B	3B	HR	RBI	BB	K	SB	CS	AVG/OBP/SLG
2018	LOU	AAA	25	202	25	12	4	5	38	20	39	10	7	.289/.373/.491
2018	CIN	MLB	25	247	27	10	1	7	31	20	60	6	1	.252/.324/.404
2019	LOU	AAA	26	172	27	8	1	6	26	19	34	6	6	.290/.384/.483
2019	CIN	MLB	26	260	30	11	7	7	23	18	63	4	3	.271/.331/.466
2020	SEA	MLB	27	47	5	3	0	0	4	8	14	0	0	.205/.340/.282
2020	CIN	MLB	27	42	5	0	0	0	0	6	8	1	0	.086/.238/.086
2021 FS	CHC	MLB	28	600	77	22	4	16	67	63	156	17	7	.225/.322/.381
2021 DC	CHC	MLB	28	65	8	2	0	1	7	6	16	1	1	.225/.322/.381

Comparables: Chuck Hinton, Curtis Pride, Al Martin

A former first-round pick, Ervin is now a 28-year-old bat-first corner outfielder coming off a season that saw his limited playing time produce worst-ever offensive results. The tools that led to him being drafted so highly still flash; however, the reason they make movies about late-bloomer comeback miracles is because they're weighed against all the times those miracles don't happen.

YEAR	TEAM	LVL	AGE	PA	DRC+	BABIP	BRR	FRAA	WARP
2018	LOU	AAA	25	202	131	.341	-0.8	LF(37): 5.2, CF(8): -0.5, RF(3): 0.3	1.3
2018	CIN	MLB	25	247	96	.310	1.0	LF(39): 0.2, RF(33): -2.7, CF(4): -0.0	0.3
2019	LOU	AAA	26	172	135	.333	2.0	CF(25): 0.9, LF(10): 1.2	1.5
2019	CIN	MLB	26	260	94	.339	1.0	LF(61): -5.5, CF(25): 1.1, RF(17): -0.7	0.2
2020	SEA	MLB	27	47	88	.320	0.3	RF(18): 0.6	0.1
2020	CIN	MLB	27	42	90	.111	0.6	LF(10): -0.8, CF(7): 0.0, RF(1): 0.1	0.0
2021 FS	CHC	MLB	28	600	98	.287	1.4	RF 0, LF 1	1.6
2021 DC	CHC	MLB	28	65	98	.287	0.2	RF 0, LF 0	0.2

Phillip Ervin, continued

Batted Ball Distribution

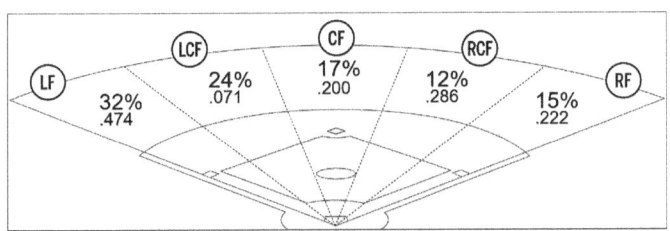

Strike Zone vs LHP   Strike Zone vs RHP

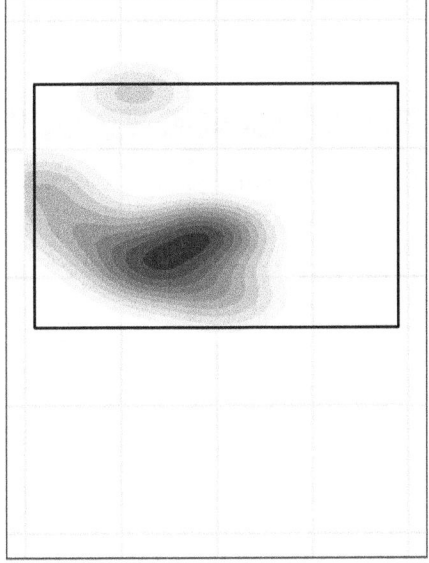

Chicago Cubs 2021

Ian Happ CF
Born: 08/12/94 Age: 26 Bats: S Throws: R
Height: 6'0" Weight: 205 Origin: Round 1, 2015 Draft (#9 overall)

YEAR	TEAM	LVL	AGE	PA	R	2B	3B	HR	RBI	BB	K	SB	CS	AVG/OBP/SLG
2018	CHC	MLB	23	462	56	19	2	15	44	70	167	8	4	.233/.353/.408
2019	IOW	AAA	24	429	66	18	1	16	53	65	113	9	2	.242/.364/.432
2019	CHC	MLB	24	156	25	7	1	11	30	15	39	2	0	.264/.333/.564
2020	CHC	MLB	25	231	27	11	1	12	28	30	63	1	3	.258/.361/.505
2021 FS	CHC	MLB	26	600	89	24	2	28	82	72	182	5	3	.242/.338/.461
2021 DC	CHC	MLB	26	590	88	24	2	27	81	71	179	5	3	.242/.338/.461

Comparables: Preston Wilson, Jose Cruz, Ramón Laureano

Happ has essentially played consecutive two-month seasons, and in each one he's performed a lot like the Cubs probably envisioned when they spent a top-10 pick on him back in 2015. The swing-and-miss in his game isn't going anywhere, but he's made a dent in it while becoming more selective overall. When he makes contact, he hits the crap out of the ball, and even though the sample sizes of the last two years are small, everything about it looks sustainable. A steadying force in a lineup whose stars of yesteryear weren't shining as brightly as we've grown accustomed, Happ looks primed to take over as the next most integral part of the Cubs' lineup.

YEAR	TEAM	LVL	AGE	PA	DRC+	BABIP	BRR	FRAA	WARP
2018	CHC	MLB	23	462	88	.362	2.0	CF(63): -7.9, LF(59): -2.5, RF(24): 0.6	-0.1
2019	IOW	AAA	24	429	99	.307	1.2	CF(79): -4.0, 2B(20): 3.1, LF(2): 0.2	1.5
2019	CHC	MLB	24	156	112	.286	1.7	LF(15): -0.4, 2B(13): -0.9, CF(13): 1.2	1.0
2020	CHC	MLB	25	231	124	.317	-2.2	CF(51): -8.6, LF(28): -0.3, RF(7): -0.4	0.2
2021 FS	CHC	MLB	26	600	117	.314	-0.1	CF -2, LF 0	2.8
2021 DC	CHC	MLB	26	590	117	.314	-0.1	CF -2, LF 0	2.7

Ian Happ, continued

Batted Ball Distribution

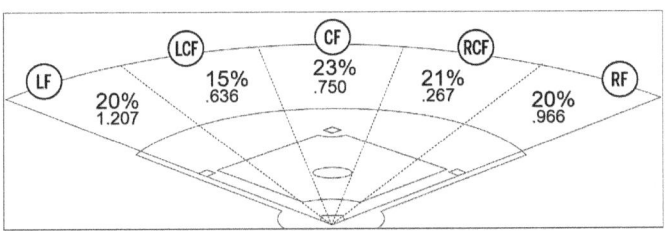

Strike Zone vs LHP   Strike Zone vs RHP

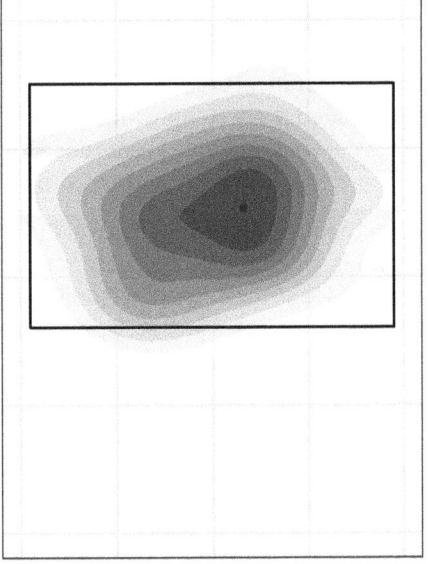

Jason Heyward RF
Born: 08/09/89 Age: 31 Bats: L Throws: L
Height: 6'5" Weight: 240 Origin: Round 1, 2007 Draft (#14 overall)

YEAR	TEAM	LVL	AGE	PA	R	2B	3B	HR	RBI	BB	K	SB	CS	AVG/OBP/SLG
2018	CHC	MLB	28	489	67	23	4	8	57	42	60	1	1	.270/.335/.395
2019	CHC	MLB	29	589	78	20	4	21	62	68	110	8	3	.251/.343/.429
2020	CHC	MLB	30	181	20	6	2	6	22	30	37	2	0	.265/.392/.456
2021 FS	CHC	MLB	31	600	75	23	3	17	73	68	117	7	4	.241/.335/.400
2021 DC	CHC	MLB	31	562	70	22	3	16	68	64	109	7	3	.241/.335/.400

Comparables: Jeff DaVanon, Michael Cuddyer, Bobby Kielty

Heyward discourse most often focuses on the $184-million contract he signed before the 2016 season and how he's failed to consistently perform at the level of a player worthy of that salary. Heyward didn't sign himself to that contract, of course, and has by every indication given his all to the Cubs' organization, even if he's failed to live up to the expectations of fans, the people who gave him that contract and, very likely, himself.

On August 26th, Heyward sat out the Cubs' game against the Tigers, joining athletes from across the country in protesting the shooting of Jacob Blake by a police officer earlier that week in Kenosha, Wis. His teammates played without him, and while everyone said the right thing—Heyward indicated that he encouraged them to play—it was a jarring decision. Even if Heyward told them to play—what else was he supposed to say?—his teammates, or even his manager, could have made the simple decision to stand with him in solidarity.

On the field, Heyward was the Cubs' best player by any definition, steadying the offense while Chicago's other top hitters slumped and/or couldn't stay healthy. He showed patience unlike we've ever seen from him before, and he hit the ball harder on average, ripping line drives all over the field while providing his usual sterling defense in right field.

Whether the adjustments Heyward made are sustainable is tough to say given the short season—line-drive rates aren't the most predictive metrics—but even if they're not, the Cubs owe him another $65 million over the final three years of his contract. Heyward, on the other hand, owes the Cubs nothing.

YEAR	TEAM	LVL	AGE	PA	DRC+	BABIP	BRR	FRAA	WARP
2018	CHC	MLB	28	489	94	.297	3.0	RF(118): 11.5, CF(25): -2.7	2.0
2019	CHC	MLB	29	589	104	.281	-0.4	RF(105): -11.3, CF(84): -1.5	0.8
2020	CHC	MLB	30	181	113	.311	2.1	RF(50): 5.8	1.5
2021 FS	CHC	MLB	31	600	102	.280	0.3	RF 2, CF 0	1.8
2021 DC	CHC	MLB	31	562	102	.280	0.2	RF 2	1.5

Jason Heyward, continued

Batted Ball Distribution

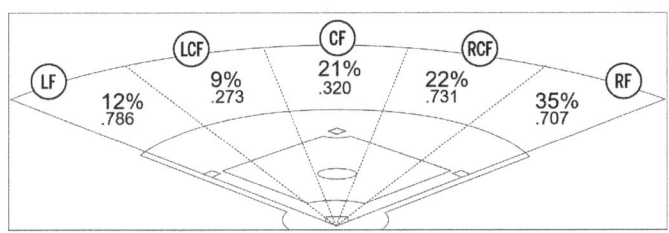

Strike Zone vs LHP   Strike Zone vs RHP

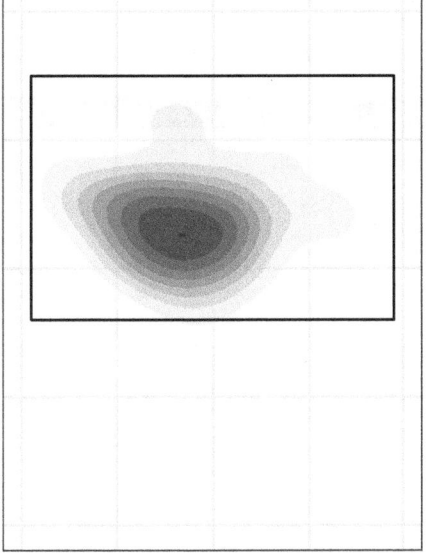

Nico Hoerner SS

Born: 05/13/97   Age: 24   Bats: R   Throws: R
Height: 6'1"   Weight: 200   Origin: Round 1, 2018 Draft (#24 overall)

YEAR	TEAM	LVL	AGE	PA	R	2B	3B	HR	RBI	BB	K	SB	CS	AVG/OBP/SLG
2018	CUBB	ROK	21	15	3	1	1	0	1	2	0	2	0	.250/.400/.500
2018	EUG	SS	21	28	6	0	1	1	2	5	3	4	1	.318/.464/.545
2018	SB	LO-A	21	17	1	1	0	1	3	2	1	0	0	.400/.471/.667
2019	CUBR	ROK	22	21	2	1	0	0	0	1	1	0	0	.400/.429/.450
2019	TNS	AA	22	294	37	16	3	3	22	21	31	8	4	.284/.344/.399
2019	CHC	MLB	22	82	13	1	1	3	17	3	11	0	0	.282/.305/.436
2020	CHC	MLB	23	126	19	4	0	0	13	12	24	3	2	.222/.312/.259
2021 FS	*CHC*	*MLB*	*24*	*600*	*71*	*24*	*3*	*13*	*68*	*44*	*110*	*5*	*3*	*.255/.319/.389*
2021 DC	*CHC*	*MLB*	*24*	*467*	*55*	*19*	*3*	*10*	*53*	*34*	*86*	*4*	*2*	*.255/.319/.389*

Comparables: Tony Taylor, Glenn Hubbard, Ryne Sandberg

It was a weird season for Hoerner, who was expected to take the mantle at second base for the Cubs. Instead, he bounced around the diamond and struggled to get his bat going. Hoerner's calling card was and continues to be his hit tool, but that has yet to show up against big-league pitching. Given that the rest of his skill set is run-of-the-mill, it's fair to say that any continuation of that theme heading forward would be concerning.

YEAR	TEAM	LVL	AGE	PA	DRC+	BABIP	BRR	FRAA	WARP
2018	CUBB	ROK	21	15		.250			
2018	EUG	SS	21	28	170	.333	-0.5	SS(5): -0.4	0.1
2018	SB	LO-A	21	17	145	.385	0.0	SS(4): -0.4	0.1
2019	CUBR	ROK	22	21		.421			
2019	TNS	AA	22	294	103	.311	1.6	SS(44): -2.6, 2B(16): 0.5, CF(11): 2.8	1.5
2019	CHC	MLB	22	82	94	.292	0.3	SS(17): 0.6, 2B(1): 0.1, CF(1): -0.1	0.4
2020	CHC	MLB	23	126	81	.279	0.8	2B(37): 3.7, SS(10): 0.5, 3B(6): -0.2	0.5
2021 FS	*CHC*	*MLB*	*24*	*600*	*95*	*.297*	*0.1*	*2B 7, CF 0*	*2.1*
2021 DC	*CHC*	*MLB*	*24*	*467*	*95*	*.297*	*0.1*	*2B 5, CF 0*	*1.6*

Nico Hoerner, continued

Batted Ball Distribution

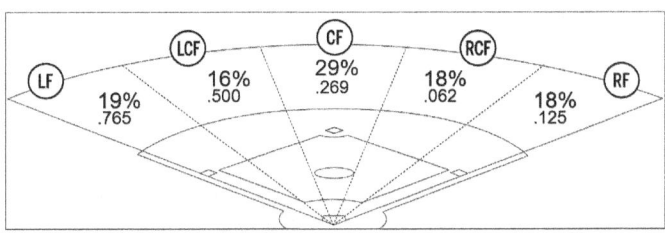

Strike Zone vs LHP   Strike Zone vs RHP

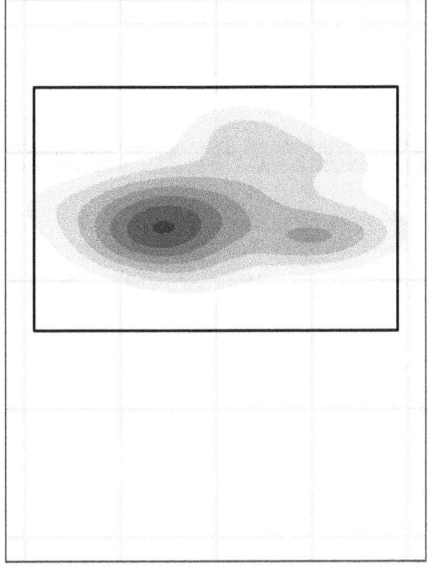

Chicago Cubs 2021

Cameron Maybin LF

Born: 04/04/87   Age: 34   Bats: R   Throws: R
Height: 6'3"   Weight: 215   Origin: Round 1, 2005 Draft (#10 overall)

YEAR	TEAM	LVL	AGE	PA	R	2B	3B	HR	RBI	BB	K	SB	CS	AVG/OBP/SLG
2018	MIA	MLB	31	287	20	12	1	3	20	32	55	8	5	.251/.338/.343
2018	SEA	MLB	31	97	12	2	1	1	8	6	20	2	0	.242/.289/.319
2019	COL	AAA	32	67	4	3	0	0	5	13	20	1	2	.216/.388/.275
2019	NYY	MLB	32	269	48	17	0	11	32	30	72	9	6	.285/.364/.494
2020	DET	MLB	33	45	5	4	0	1	2	4	13	0	0	.244/.311/.415
2020	CHC	MLB	33	56	3	4	1	0	5	3	12	3	0	.250/.304/.365
2021 FS	CHC	MLB	34	600	58	24	1	12	59	59	148	22	9	.229/.311/.353
2021 DC	CHC	MLB	34	239	23	9	0	5	23	23	59	8	4	.229/.311/.353

Comparables: Carlos Gómez, Alejandro De Aza, Jerry Martin

Maybin has been acquired by nine teams since the start of 2017. He ended last season with the Cubs, having been traded by the Tigers at the deadline; it was the third time Detroit—and Detroit alone—had dealt him. He probably thought he was done with this nomadic lifestyle nonsense after he did a superb job filling in for an injury-ravaged Yankees team in 2019, but that stability (and his performance in pinstripes) looks to be an outlier. Wherever Maybin ends up, don't get too comfortable with seeing him there; he'll likely be on the move again before long.

YEAR	TEAM	LVL	AGE	PA	DRC+	BABIP	BRR	FRAA	WARP
2018	MIA	MLB	31	287	88	.308	-2.7	LF(44): 2.1, CF(30): -0.7, RF(24): -0.1	0.3
2018	SEA	MLB	31	97	88	.300	-0.2	CF(20): -1.6, LF(12): 0.4	0.0
2019	COL	AAA	32	67	128	.344	-1.9	CF(5): -0.3, LF(4): -0.2, RF(2): -0.1	0.2
2019	NYY	MLB	32	269	105	.365	-1.0	LF(46): -0.5, RF(36): 0.7, CF(3): 0.4	0.9
2020	DET	MLB	33	45	86	.333	-0.1	RF(12): -0.3	-0.1
2020	CHC	MLB	33	56	83	.325	-0.2	RF(7): 0.5, LF(5): 0.2, CF(4): -0.5	0.0
2021 FS	CHC	MLB	34	600	84	.293	1.5	CF 0, RF 1	0.6
2021 DC	CHC	MLB	34	239	84	.293	0.6	CF 0, RF 0	0.2

Cameron Maybin, continued

Batted Ball Distribution

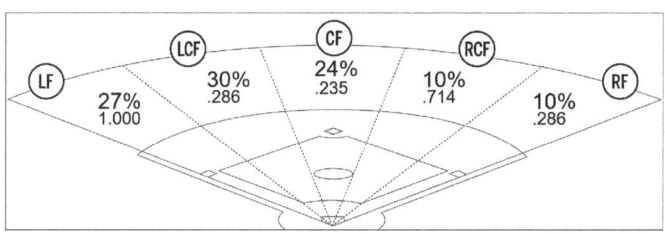

Strike Zone vs LHP   **Strike Zone vs RHP**

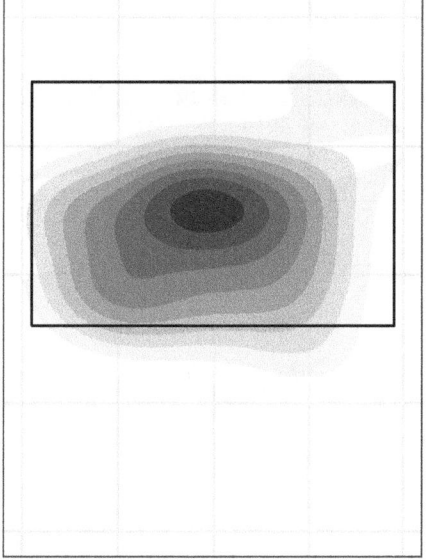

Chicago Cubs 2021

Joc Pederson LF

Born: 04/21/92   Age: 29   Bats: L   Throws: L
Height: 6'1"   Weight: 220   Origin: Round 11, 2010 Draft (#352 overall)

YEAR	TEAM	LVL	AGE	PA	R	2B	3B	HR	RBI	BB	K	SB	CS	AVG/OBP/SLG
2018	LAD	MLB	26	443	65	27	3	25	56	40	85	1	5	.248/.321/.522
2019	LAD	MLB	27	514	83	16	3	36	74	50	111	1	1	.249/.339/.538
2020	LAD	MLB	28	138	21	4	0	7	16	11	34	1	0	.190/.285/.397
2021 FS	CHC	MLB	29	600	94	25	2	32	83	72	156	5	3	.236/.345/.482
2021 DC	CHC	MLB	29	485	76	20	1	26	67	58	126	4	2	.236/.345/.482

Comparables: Rick Ankiel, Don Lock, Preston Wilson

A hole opened up in Pederson's swing in 2020, across the top of the strike zone, and the shortened season prevented him from closing it. The swings and misses on elevated pitches reflected issues that also led to more pulled ground balls, allowing shifts to devour much of his usual production. In the postseason though, he got hot, reminding everyone how much upside there is in a patient lefty slugger with good power. He's strictly a corner outfielder at this point, and not a terrific one, but when he works the count and gets his pitch, he can drive it consistently enough to be a solid regular. His pop is ballpark-proof, too; he hits the kind of homers that no deep right field can turn into flyouts.

YEAR	TEAM	LVL	AGE	PA	DRC+	BABIP	BRR	FRAA	WARP
2018	LAD	MLB	26	443	117	.253	0.9	LF(116): -1.3, CF(32): -2.4, RF(2): -0.1	1.9
2019	LAD	MLB	27	514	122	.249	2.6	LF(84): 0.5, RF(39): -0.0, 1B(20): -1.0	3.0
2020	LAD	MLB	28	138	91	.200	-0.6	LF(23): -0.5, RF(8): 0.9	0.2
2021 FS	CHC	MLB	29	600	123	.274	-0.2	LF 0, 1B 0	3.2
2021 DC	CHC	MLB	29	485	123	.274	-0.2	LF 0	2.5

Joc Pederson, continued

Batted Ball Distribution

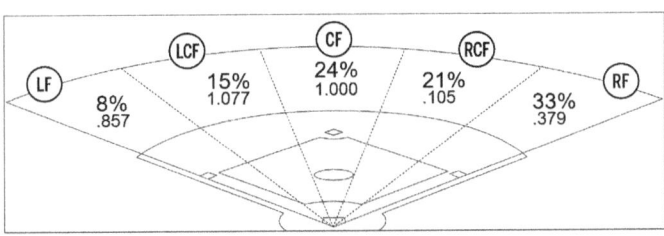

Strike Zone vs LHP   Strike Zone vs RHP

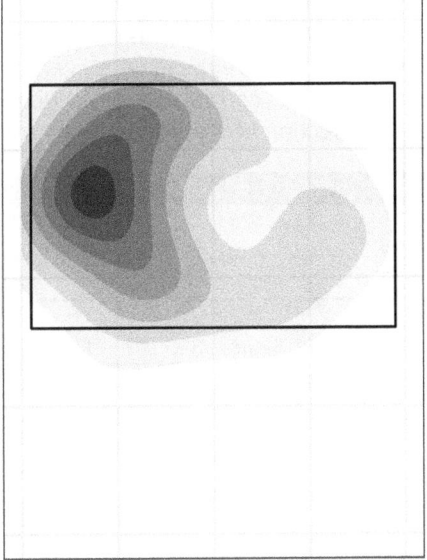

Anthony Rizzo 1B

Born: 08/08/89 Age: 31 Bats: L Throws: L
Height: 6'3" Weight: 240 Origin: Round 6, 2007 Draft (#204 overall)

YEAR	TEAM	LVL	AGE	PA	R	2B	3B	HR	RBI	BB	K	SB	CS	AVG/OBP/SLG
2018	CHC	MLB	28	665	74	29	1	25	101	70	80	6	4	.283/.376/.470
2019	CHC	MLB	29	613	89	29	3	27	94	71	86	5	2	.293/.405/.520
2020	CHC	MLB	30	243	26	6	0	11	24	28	38	3	1	.222/.342/.414
2021 FS	CHC	MLB	31	600	97	25	2	27	87	71	101	6	3	.261/.379/.487
2021 DC	CHC	MLB	31	609	99	25	2	28	88	72	103	6	3	.261/.379/.487

Comparables: Boog Powell, Jason Thompson, Willie Aikens

Rizzo accomplished an incredibly rare feat in 2020: He got the Cubs to spend more money than they were required. After all, the $16.5 million team option that was exercised for the last year of his deal didn't have to be spent on baseball—it could have been given to organizations hellbent on denying basic human rights. Maybe it was that Rizzo's performance has been so consistent, and his approval rating so high with the Chicago fans, that even the Ricketts family didn't want to suffer the PR hit that letting him walk for nothing would have inspired. While Rizzo did suffer some decline, it wasn't in the same stratosphere as some of his compatriots; his career-worst DRC+ still rested comfortably above the league-average mark. A gambling man wouldn't wager on the Ricketts continuing to pay Rizzo after 2021—whatever the reason—but even in decline he should remain a reasonably productive first baseman.

YEAR	TEAM	LVL	AGE	PA	DRC+	BABIP	BRR	FRAA	WARP
2018	CHC	MLB	28	665	128	.287	-5.8	1B(153): 14.4, 2B(1): -0.0, P(1): -0.0	4.1
2019	CHC	MLB	29	613	135	.306	-4.9	1B(146): 4.4	3.7
2020	CHC	MLB	30	243	123	.218	-1.2	1B(57): -3.2	0.6
2021 FS	CHC	MLB	31	600	136	.278	-0.2	1B 2, 2B 0	3.8
2021 DC	CHC	MLB	31	609	136	.278	-0.2	1B 2	3.9

Anthony Rizzo, continued

Batted Ball Distribution

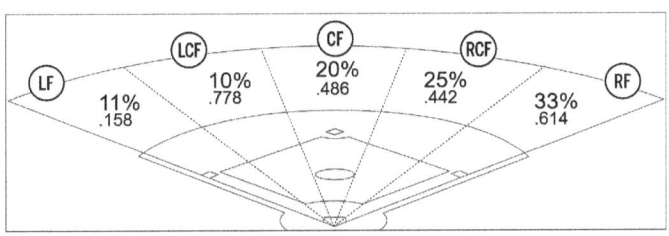

Strike Zone vs LHP   Strike Zone vs RHP

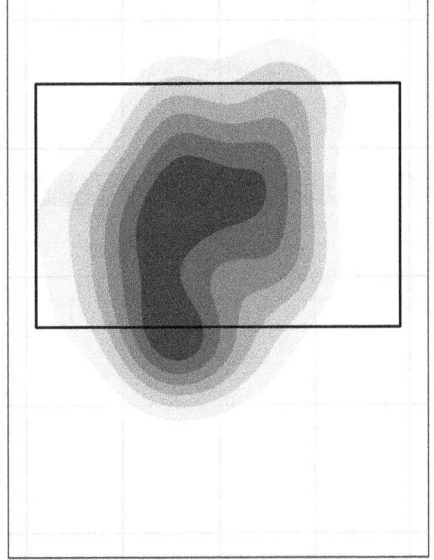

Chicago Cubs 2021

Austin Romine   C
Born: 11/22/88   Age: 32   Bats: R   Throws: R
Height: 6'1"   Weight: 216   Origin: Round 2, 2007 Draft (#94 overall)

YEAR	TEAM	LVL	AGE	PA	R	2B	3B	HR	RBI	BB	K	SB	CS	AVG/OBP/SLG
2018	NYY	MLB	29	265	30	12	0	10	42	17	67	1	0	.244/.295/.417
2019	NYY	MLB	30	240	29	12	0	8	35	10	50	1	1	.281/.310/.439
2020	DET	MLB	31	135	12	5	0	2	17	4	47	0	0	.238/.259/.323
2021 FS	CHC	MLB	32	600	66	23	1	16	69	33	173	2	2	.219/.267/.353
2021 DC	CHC	MLB	32	156	17	6	0	4	18	8	45	0	1	.219/.267/.353

Comparables: Humberto Quintero, Robert Machado, Damon Berryhill

There's something wildly psychotic about growing huge swaths of facial hair during hot summers in a job that requires extra headgear, but it probably stems from overcompensating for years of Yankees paychecks. So the verdict is in: Romine, a reliable backup catcher, is now a certified Beard Guy as well. He also has a history with Miguel Cabrera, getting into a shoving match during a 2017 game as opponents, then voluntarily spending a year as teammates. This also shows he's able to bury the hatchet, and in needing a location for it, could explain the heavy beard.

YEAR	TEAM	P. COUNT	FRM RUNS	BLK RUNS	THRW RUNS	TOT RUNS
2018	NYY	10494	4.2	2.2	0.0	6.3
2019	NYY	9536	-2.2	0.9	0.1	-1.1
2020	DET	5408	-0.7	0.2	0.3	-0.2
2021	CHC	6012	-0.5	0.0	-0.6	-1.1
2021	CHC	6012	-0.5	-0.1	-0.6	-1.2

YEAR	TEAM	LVL	AGE	PA	DRC+	BABIP	BRR	FRAA	WARP
2018	NYY	MLB	29	265	85	.292	-3.1	C(76): 6.8	1.2
2019	NYY	MLB	30	240	89	.327	-1.0	C(70): -2.5, P(1): -0.0	0.6
2020	DET	MLB	31	135	51	.354	-0.9	C(37): -0.6, 1B(1): 0.2	-0.5
2021 FS	CHC	MLB	32	600	66	.287	-0.6	C -4, 1B 0	-0.6
2021 DC	CHC	MLB	32	156	66	.287	-0.1	C -1	-0.2

Austin Romine, continued

Batted Ball Distribution

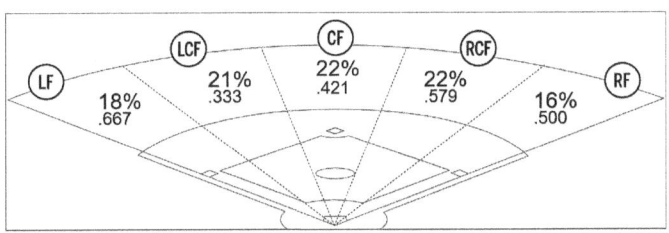

Strike Zone vs LHP   Strike Zone vs RHP

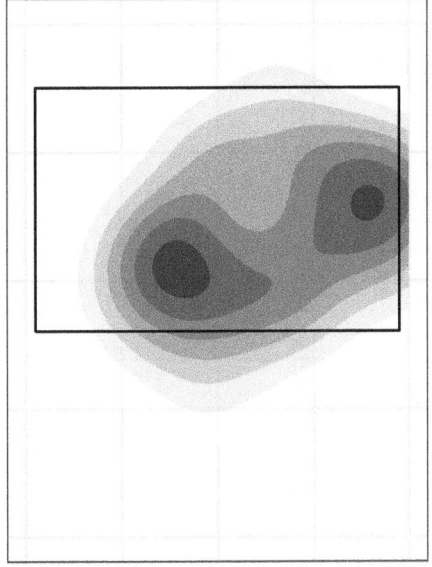

Ildemaro Vargas 2B

Born: 07/16/91 Age: 29 Bats: S Throws: R
Height: 6'0" Weight: 180 Origin: International Free Agent, 2008

YEAR	TEAM	LVL	AGE	PA	R	2B	3B	HR	RBI	BB	K	SB	CS	AVG/OBP/SLG
2018	RNO	AAA	26	572	78	31	10	7	54	30	46	10	4	.311/.348/.445
2018	ARI	MLB	26	20	2	0	0	1	4	1	4	1	0	.211/.250/.368
2019	RNO	AAA	27	137	20	9	3	2	24	11	5	1	1	.403/.453/.573
2019	ARI	MLB	27	211	25	9	1	6	24	9	24	1	0	.269/.299/.413
2020	ARI	MLB	28	21	2	0	0	0	0	1	5	0	0	.150/.190/.150
2020	MIN	MLB	28	24	3	1	1	0	2	1	2	0	0	.227/.250/.364
2020	CHC	MLB	28	9	1	0	0	1	1	0	3	0	0	.222/.222/.556
2021 FS	CHC	MLB	29	600	68	26	3	12	69	34	85	1	1	.258/.307/.384
2021 DC	CHC	MLB	29	132	15	5	0	2	15	7	18	0	0	.258/.307/.384

Comparables: Carlos Garcia, Jerry Adair, Omar Infante

Vargas' home run off Josh Hader in the ninth inning of the Cubs' comeback win over the Brewers on Sept. 12 was one of the least likely of the season. The rest of Vargas' campaign featured zero home runs, nine hits and three different franchises for which he suited up.

YEAR	TEAM	LVL	AGE	PA	DRC+	BABIP	BRR	FRAA	WARP
2018	RNO	AAA	26	572	99	.329	-3.8	SS(107): -6.0, 2B(17): -0.1	0.7
2018	ARI	MLB	26	20	93	.214	0.0	3B(3): 0.3, 2B(2): 0.1, SS(1): -0.0	0.1
2019	RNO	AAA	27	137	144	.407	1.9	SS(13): 0.8, 3B(12): 0.3, 2B(6): 0.4	1.6
2019	ARI	MLB	27	211	87	.279	0.4	2B(48): 2.4, 3B(14): -1.1, SS(4): 0.5	0.6
2020	ARI	MLB	28	21	79	.200	0.2	1B(5): -0.3, 2B(3): 0.2, 3B(1): -0.1	0.0
2020	MIN	MLB	28	24	82	.238	-0.7	2B(8): 0.8, 3B(1): 0.0	0.0
2020	CHC	MLB	28	9	75	.200		2B(5): 0.4, 3B(1): -0.0	0.0
2021 FS	CHC	MLB	29	600	88	.286	-0.4	2B 2, SS 0	1.0
2021 DC	CHC	MLB	29	132	88	.286	-0.1	2B 0, SS 0	0.2

Ildemaro Vargas, continued

Batted Ball Distribution

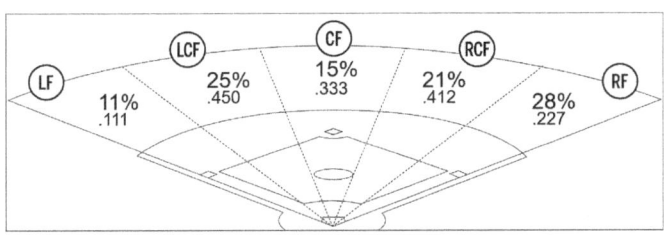

Strike Zone vs LHP   Strike Zone vs RHP

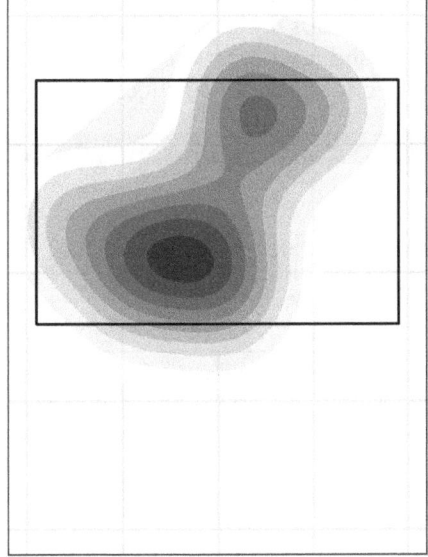

Jason Adam   RHP

Born: 08/04/91   Age: 29   Bats: R   Throws: R
Height: 6'3"   Weight: 229   Origin: Round 5, 2010 Draft (#149 overall)

YEAR	TEAM	LVL	AGE	W	L	SV	G	GS	IP	H	HR	BB/9	K/9	K	GB%	BABIP
2018	NWA	AA	26	1	0	0	6	0	11^1	5	0	3.2	13.5	17	36.4%	.227
2018	OMA	AAA	26	2	0	4	11	0	12^2	6	0	5.0	10.7	15	31.0%	.214
2018	KC	MLB	26	0	3	0	31	0	32^1	30	9	4.2	10.3	37	28.7%	.269
2019	BUF	AAA	27	1	3	1	11	0	14	10	2	3.2	12.9	20	16.1%	.276
2019	TOR	MLB	27	3	0	0	23	0	21^2	15	1	4.2	7.5	18	26.7%	.237
2020	CHC	MLB	28	2	1	0	13	0	13^2	9	2	5.3	13.8	21	37.9%	.259
2021 FS	CHC	MLB	29	2	2	0	57	0	50	40	8	4.6	11.0	61	31.4%	.274
2021 DC	CHC	MLB	29	2	2	0	51	0	42.3	34	7	4.6	11.0	52	31.4%	.274

Comparables: Juan Minaya, Austin Brice, Glenn Sparkman

Adam is a walking Johnny Cash song, with Chicago his fourth stop that was featured in "I've Been Everywhere." And with a new slider that induced whiffs nearly a quarter of the time, it could be the last one (Baltimore and its promise of black attire is still out there, after all). A low-leverage arm during his previous major-league chances in Kansas City and Toronto, Adam got more opportunities with the Cubs thanks to some bullpen injuries and inconsistencies, and while his command was sometimes erratic, he missed bats with enough regularity to make one confident his success was more than a small-sample aberration.

YEAR	TEAM	LVL	AGE	WHIP	ERA	DRA-	WARP	MPH	FB%	WHF	CSP
2018	NWA	AA	26	0.79	1.59	79	0.1				
2018	OMA	AAA	26	1.03	1.42	56	0.4				
2018	KC	MLB	26	1.39	6.12	157	-0.8	96.0	61.1%	26.4%	
2019	BUF	AAA	27	1.07	2.57	68	0.4				
2019	TOR	MLB	27	1.15	2.91	130	-0.2	95.9	61.5%	27.8%	
2020	CHC	MLB	28	1.24	3.29	85	0.2	96.5	53.8%	41.7%	
2021 FS	CHC	MLB	29	1.32	4.15	95	0.4	96.1	58.6%	32.5%	42.6%
2021 DC	CHC	MLB	29	1.32	4.15	95	0.3	96.1	58.6%	32.5%	42.6%

Jason Adam, continued

Pitch Shape vs LHH

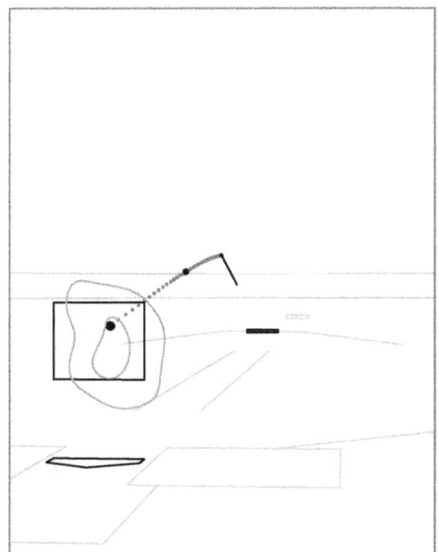

Pitch Shape vs RHH

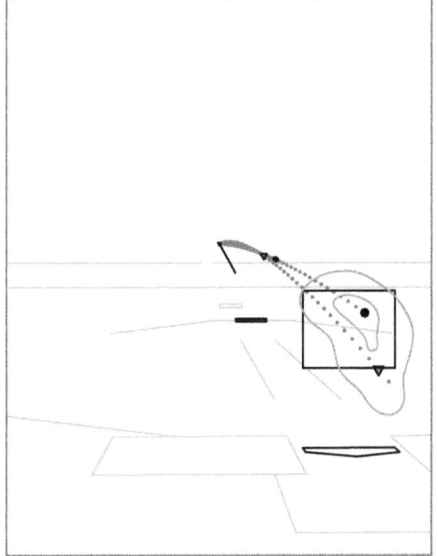

Type	Frequency	Velocity	H Movement	V Movement
● Fastball	53.8%	94.9 [107]	-6.5 [101]	-13.5 [105]
▲ Changeup	15.0%	89.8 [118]	-14.1 [88]	-28.1 [98]
▽ Slider	20.8%	82.7 [94]	6.9 [106]	-43 [73]
◇ Curveball	10.4%	79.4 [103]	10.8 [113]	-51.8 [92]

Chicago Cubs 2021

Adbert Alzolay RHP
Born: 03/01/95   Age: 26   Bats: R   Throws: R
Height: 6'1"   Weight: 208   Origin: International Free Agent, 2012

YEAR	TEAM	LVL	AGE	W	L	SV	G	GS	IP	H	HR	BB/9	K/9	K	GB%	BABIP
2018	IOW	AAA	23	2	4	0	8	8	39²	43	4	2.9	6.1	27	35.1%	.310
2019	IOW	AAA	24	2	4	0	15	15	65¹	53	10	4.3	12.5	91	32.1%	.295
2019	CHC	MLB	24	1	1	0	4	2	12¹	13	4	6.6	9.5	13	32.4%	.273
2020	CHC	MLB	25	1	1	0	6	4	21¹	12	1	5.5	12.2	29	43.2%	.256
2021 FS	CHC	MLB	26	9	8	0	26	26	150	136	25	4.5	10.1	167	35.5%	.292
2021 DC	CHC	MLB	26	5	5	0	22	16	81	73	13	4.5	10.1	90	35.5%	.292

Comparables: Alex Reyes, Walker Lockett, Jake Faria

What is Adbert Alzolay? That's not a Jeopardy! answer, but something the Cubs have been asking themselves for many moons now. The 2020 season didn't do a lot to answer that question, as he ping-ponged in and out of the rotation, finding moderate success but failing to prove he can turn a lineup over multiple times. In an age where pitching roles and usages are becoming more blurred, maybe the answer is to use him as a Daily Double—or, at least, someone who works two times through the order regardless of when they enter, a la Ryan Yarbrough. Given that Alzolay is now out of options, the Final Jeopardy phase of a player's career, the Cubs will have to submit their answer (preferably not in the form of a question) soon.

YEAR	TEAM	LVL	AGE	WHIP	ERA	DRA-	WARP	MPH	FB%	WHF	CSP
2018	IOW	AAA	23	1.41	4.76	88	0.6				
2019	IOW	AAA	24	1.29	4.41	55	2.5				
2019	CHC	MLB	24	1.78	7.30	113	0.0	95.8	57.3%	26.7%	
2020	CHC	MLB	25	1.17	2.95	85	0.4	96.5	52.2%	27.5%	
2021 FS	CHC	MLB	26	1.41	4.54	101	1.3	96.3	53.6%	27.3%	45.8%
2021 DC	CHC	MLB	26	1.41	4.54	101	0.6	96.3	53.6%	27.3%	45.8%

Adbert Alzolay, continued

Pitch Shape vs LHH

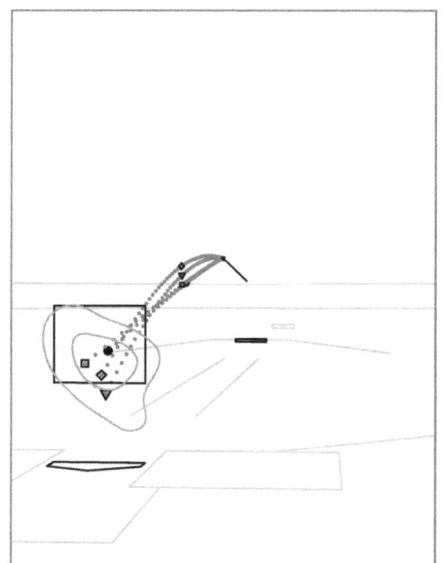

Pitch Shape vs RHH

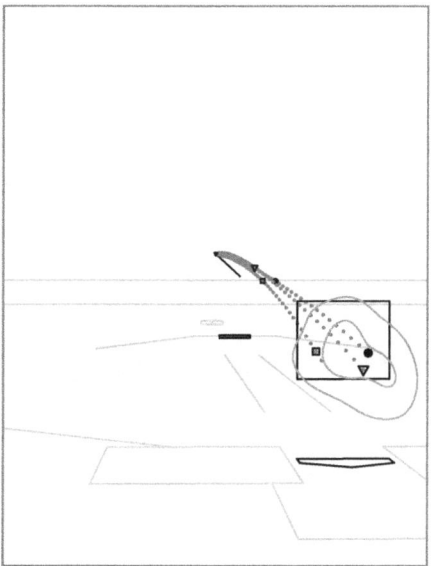

Type	Frequency	Velocity	H Movement	V Movement
● Fastball	32.0%	94.6 [106]	-7.7 [95]	-12.5 [108]
☐ Sinker	20.2%	94.9 [113]	-13.6 [96]	-16.6 [113]
▲ Changeup	8.0%	85.2 [100]	-12.6 [95]	-25 [107]
▽ Slider	24.5%	82.6 [94]	10.3 [119]	-34.8 [97]
◇ Curveball	15.2%	80.1 [106]	10.4 [111]	-41.1 [116]

Chicago Cubs 2021

Andrew Chafin   LHP

Born: 06/17/90   Age: 31   Bats: R   Throws: L
Height: 6'2"   Weight: 235   Origin: Round 1, 2011 Draft (#43 overall)

YEAR	TEAM	LVL	AGE	W	L	SV	G	GS	IP	H	HR	BB/9	K/9	K	GB%	BABIP
2018	ARI	MLB	28	1	6	0	77	0	49^1	41	0	4.6	9.7	53	50.4%	.313
2019	ARI	MLB	29	2	2	0	77	0	52^2	52	6	3.1	11.6	68	41.6%	.359
2020	CHC	MLB	30	1	2	1	15	0	9^2	11	2	4.7	12.1	13	40.7%	.360
2021 FS	CHC	MLB	31	2	2	0	57	0	50	43	6	4.3	10.6	58	46.7%	.298
2021 DC	CHC	MLB	31	1	1	0	35	0	30	26	3	4.3	10.6	35	46.7%	.298

Comparables: Alex Colomé, Jeff Manship, Luis Avilán

Chafin was limited by a sprained finger to too few appearances to get a read on if the lefty could be relied upon to get right-handed hitters out on a regular basis in the three-batter-minimum era. The small sample wasn't promising, however, as the Sheriff allowed a .937 OPS to righties in 21 plate appearances.

YEAR	TEAM	LVL	AGE	WHIP	ERA	DRA-	WARP	MPH	FB%	WHF	CSP
2018	ARI	MLB	28	1.34	3.10	94	0.4	95.2	56.6%	32.3%	
2019	ARI	MLB	29	1.33	3.76	79	0.8	95.5	61.1%	34.2%	
2020	CHC	MLB	30	1.66	6.52	87	0.2	95.1	73.4%	26.0%	
2021 FS	CHC	MLB	31	1.34	3.87	89	0.5	95.3	62.0%	32.3%	44.8%
2021 DC	CHC	MLB	31	1.34	3.87	89	0.3	95.3	62.0%	32.3%	44.8%

Andrew Chafin, continued

Pitch Shape vs LHH

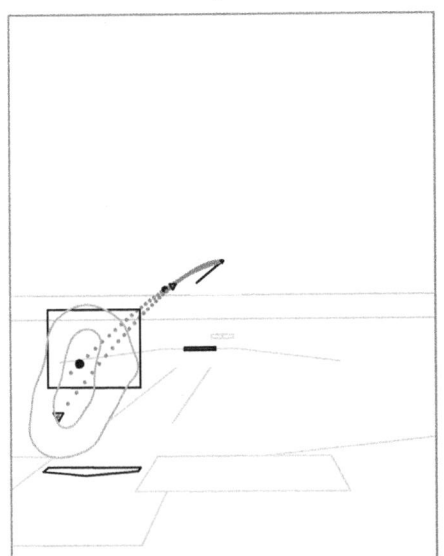

Pitch Shape vs RHH

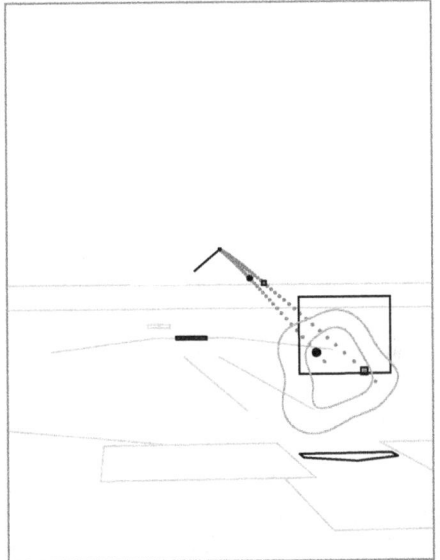

Type	Frequency	Velocity	H Movement	V Movement
● Fastball	42.6%	93.7 [103]	8 [94]	-14.6 [102]
□ Sinker	29.3%	93.5 [106]	12.6 [103]	-17.5 [110]
▽ Slider	26.1%	84 [100]	-1 [84]	-35.1 [96]

Zach Davies   RHP

Born: 02/07/93   Age: 28   Bats: R   Throws: R
Height: 6'0"   Weight: 180   Origin: Round 26, 2011 Draft (#785 overall)

YEAR	TEAM	LVL	AGE	W	L	SV	G	GS	IP	H	HR	BB/9	K/9	K	GB%	BABIP
2018	WIS	LO-A	25	1	0	0	4	4	19	19	2	0.0	9.0	19	62.7%	.347
2018	BLX	AA	25	1	1	0	2	2	11	7	1	3.3	9.8	12	50.0%	.250
2018	RMV	AAA	25	0	3	0	5	5	17	18	0	6.4	6.9	13	40.7%	.340
2018	MIL	MLB	25	2	7	0	13	13	66	67	8	2.9	6.7	49	47.1%	.299
2019	MIL	MLB	26	10	7	0	31	31	159^2	155	20	2.9	5.7	102	39.1%	.276
2020	SD	MLB	27	7	4	0	12	12	69^1	55	9	2.5	8.2	63	40.7%	.250
2021 FS	CHC	MLB	28	9	8	0	26	26	150	144	23	3.3	8.0	132	42.8%	.285
2021 DC	CHC	MLB	28	9	8	0	27	27	151.3	145	23	3.3	8.0	134	42.8%	.285

Comparables: Jair Jurrjens, Jonathon Niese, John Danks

Davies enjoyed a career year in San Diego after coming over from Milwaukee as part of the Luis Urías trade, and it might not be a fluke. He started throwing his changeup more while significantly decreasing the use of his sinker. (He threw his cutter a little more, too.) Shocker: Davies throwing his best pitch more worked out pretty well, with opposing batters whiffing on it about 35 percent of the time. Speaking of whiffs, Davies' once paltry strikeout rate shot up to about 23 percent, which was still below average but closer to respectable. The improved bat-missing ability allowed him to give the Padres some much-needed quality innings. It's worth pointing out that he did benefit from some BABIP luck, so his 2.73 ERA is a bit deceptive. Davies, now entering his walk year, can only hope that continues.

YEAR	TEAM	LVL	AGE	WHIP	ERA	DRA-	WARP	MPH	FB%	WHF	CSP
2018	WIS	LO-A	25	1.00	2.84	60	0.5				
2018	BLX	AA	25	1.00	4.09	42	0.4				
2018	RMV	AAA	25	1.76	6.35	100	0.2				
2018	MIL	MLB	25	1.33	4.77	104	0.5	91.8	56.4%	20.3%	
2019	MIL	MLB	26	1.29	3.55	108	0.8	90.2	52.4%	17.2%	
2020	SD	MLB	27	1.07	2.73	94	0.9	90.3	39.1%	25.6%	
2021 FS	CHC	MLB	28	1.33	4.19	96	1.8	90.4	48.4%	20.4%	41.7%
2021 DC	CHC	MLB	28	1.33	4.19	96	1.8	90.4	48.4%	20.4%	41.7%

Zach Davies, continued

Pitch Shape vs LHH

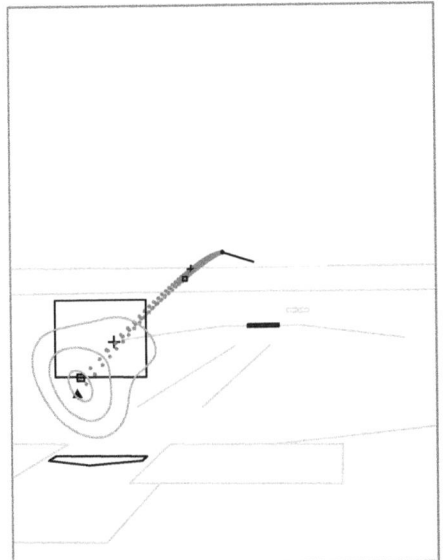

Pitch Shape vs RHH

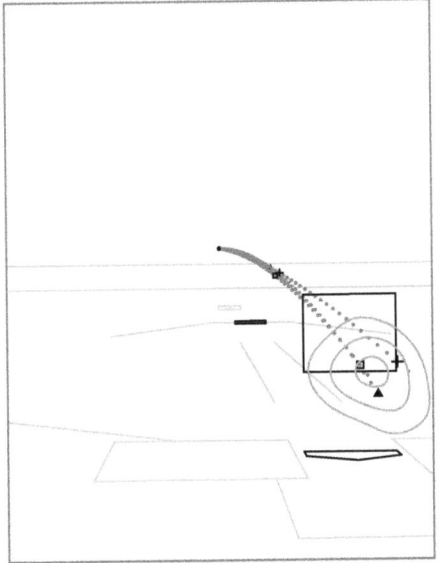

Type	Frequency	Velocity	H Movement	V Movement
☐ Sinker	39.1%	88.5 [80]	-13.1 [99]	-20.2 [101]
+ Cutter	16.7%	87.1 [92]	-5.1 [54]	-19.8 [117]
▲ Changeup	41.3%	79.4 [78]	-12.7 [95]	-31.7 [89]

Kyle Hendricks   RHP

Born: 12/07/89   Age: 31   Bats: R   Throws: R
Height: 6'3"   Weight: 190   Origin: Round 8, 2011 Draft (#264 overall)

YEAR	TEAM	LVL	AGE	W	L	SV	G	GS	IP	H	HR	BB/9	K/9	K	GB%	BABIP
2018	CHC	MLB	28	14	11	0	33	33	199	184	22	2.0	7.3	161	46.3%	.285
2019	CHC	MLB	29	11	10	0	30	30	177	168	19	1.6	7.6	150	41.1%	.292
2020	CHC	MLB	30	6	5	0	12	12	81^1	73	10	0.9	7.1	64	47.1%	.272
2021 FS	CHC	MLB	31	10	7	0	26	26	150	144	21	1.8	7.7	127	45.4%	.286
2021 DC	CHC	MLB	31	12	8	0	29	29	177.7	171	25	1.8	7.7	151	45.4%	.286

Comparables: David Price, Tom Seaver, James Shields

In 2014, a program named Eugene Goostman, which simulates a 13-year-old Ukrainian boy, reportedly passed the Turing test at an event organized by the University of Reading, although many disputed the results. Similarly, in 2018, a Google Duplex reservation system made a phone call to a hair salon to schedule an appointment for a haircut. Whether or not the Turing test has truly been passed is unknown, but that's mostly because it hasn't been given to Hendricks, who you might well suspect is a robot; not in some crazy, Westworld-esque way, just in the dull, reliable manner that you'd find on an assembly line. All Hendricks does is go to work, start after start, year after year and puts up consistent numbers without much drama or exception. We'd say it's boring, but it's a pretty exciting proposition if you're his engineer—er, we mean his manager.

YEAR	TEAM	LVL	AGE	WHIP	ERA	DRA-	WARP	MPH	FB%	WHF	CSP
2018	CHC	MLB	28	1.15	3.44	69	5.0	88.4	61.8%	22.0%	
2019	CHC	MLB	29	1.13	3.46	79	3.6	88.6	62.2%	22.1%	
2020	CHC	MLB	30	1.00	2.88	88	1.3	89.1	55.0%	24.7%	
2021 FS	CHC	MLB	31	1.16	3.48	84	2.8	88.7	60.0%	22.8%	50.4%
2021 DC	CHC	MLB	31	1.16	3.48	84	3.3	88.7	60.0%	22.8%	50.4%

Kyle Hendricks, continued

Pitch Shape vs LHH

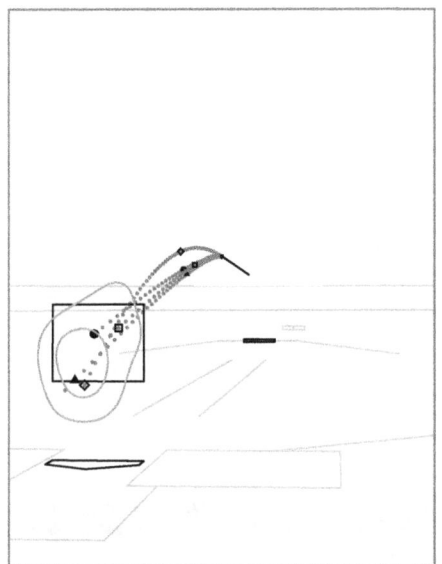

Pitch Shape vs RHH

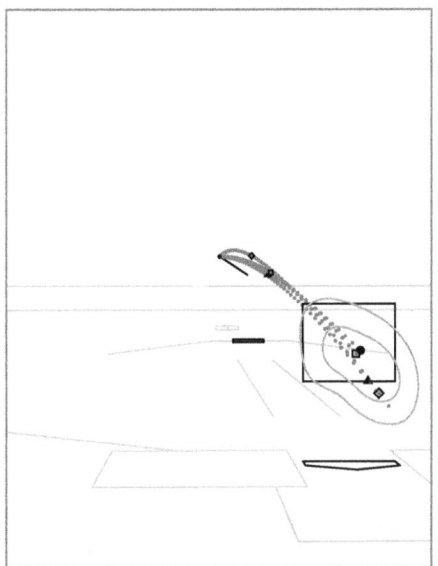

Type	Frequency	Velocity	H Movement	V Movement
● Fastball	21.0%	87.6 [84]	-5.3 [107]	-18.4 [91]
☐ Sinker	33.2%	87.5 [74]	-11.2 [114]	-23.3 [91]
▲ Changeup	27.9%	79.9 [79]	-10.2 [108]	-27.8 [99]
◇ Curveball	16.5%	72.3 [75]	12.8 [121]	-59.6 [75]

Chicago Cubs 2021

Jonathan Holder   RHP
Born: 06/09/93   Age: 28   Bats: R   Throws: R
Height: 6'2"   Weight: 232   Origin: Round 6, 2014 Draft (#182 overall)

YEAR	TEAM	LVL	AGE	W	L	SV	G	GS	IP	H	HR	BB/9	K/9	K	GB%	BABIP
2018	SWB	AAA	25	1	0	0	4	1	6	5	1	1.5	12.0	8	53.3%	.286
2018	NYY	MLB	25	1	3	0	60	1	66	53	4	2.6	8.2	60	29.2%	.263
2019	SWB	AAA	26	1	1	2	9	0	12^1	13	1	1.5	10.9	15	45.7%	.364
2019	NYY	MLB	26	5	2	0	34	1	41^1	43	8	2.4	10.0	46	38.5%	.307
2020	NYY	MLB	27	3	0	0	18	0	21^2	25	3	4.6	5.8	14	50.0%	.301
2021 FS	CHC	MLB	28	2	2	0	57	0	50	45	7	2.7	8.5	47	40.8%	.280
2021 DC	CHC	MLB	28	1	1	0	28	0	30	27	4	2.7	8.5	28	40.8%	.280

Comparables: Phil Maton, Dominic Leone, Dan Altavilla

Holder continues to occupy a spot on a team's 40-man roster despite a plummeting strikeout rate, a spike in walks, loss of control and an ERA north of 5.00 for the second consecutive season. All of which tells us a lot more about teams' needs to fill innings than anything else. You might just say that utility is in the eye of Holder's employer. That employer as of press time was the Cubs, who signed him to a non-guaranteed deal after he fell out of favor with the Yankees.

YEAR	TEAM	LVL	AGE	WHIP	ERA	DRA-	WARP	MPH	FB%	WHF	CSP
2018	SWB	AAA	25	1.00	3.00	55	0.2				
2018	NYY	MLB	25	1.09	3.14	96	0.5	94.2	55.4%	24.1%	
2019	SWB	AAA	26	1.22	2.92	66	0.4				
2019	NYY	MLB	26	1.31	6.31	96	0.3	93.8	54.5%	25.7%	
2020	NYY	MLB	27	1.66	4.98	104	0.1	93.4	52.4%	24.1%	
2021 FS	CHC	MLB	28	1.20	3.57	85	0.6	93.8	54.0%	24.7%	47.5%
2021 DC	CHC	MLB	28	1.20	3.57	85	0.4	93.8	54.0%	24.7%	47.5%

Jonathan Holder, continued

Pitch Shape vs LHH

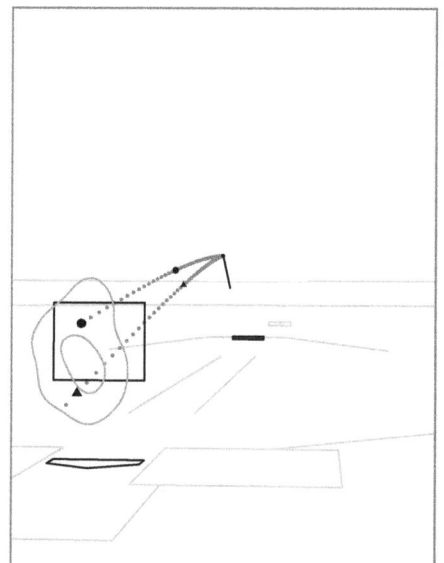

Pitch Shape vs RHH

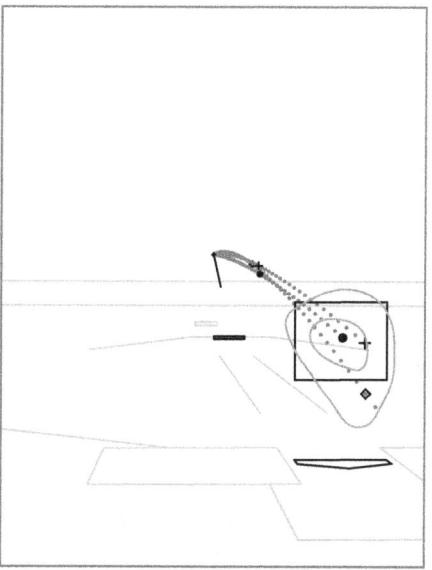

Type	Frequency	Velocity	H Movement	V Movement
● Fastball	51.9%	92.2 [99]	-2.9 [118]	-13.9 [104]
+ Cutter	9.7%	87.4 [94]	5.5 [123]	-26.6 [91]
▲ Changeup	23.9%	87.4 [109]	-12.9 [93]	-24.5 [108]
◇ Curveball	13.2%	80 [105]	7.1 [98]	-47.7 [102]

Chicago Cubs 2021

Jeremy Jeffress   RHP
Born: 09/21/87   Age: 33   Bats: R   Throws: R
Height: 6'0"   Weight: 205   Origin: Round 1, 2006 Draft (#16 overall)

YEAR	TEAM	LVL	AGE	W	L	SV	G	GS	IP	H	HR	BB/9	K/9	K	GB%	BABIP
2018	MIL	MLB	30	8	1	15	73	0	76²	49	5	3.2	10.4	89	57.7%	.250
2019	MIL	MLB	31	3	4	1	48	0	52	54	5	2.9	8.0	46	47.8%	.327
2020	CHC	MLB	32	4	1	8	22	0	23¹	10	1	4.6	6.6	17	54.4%	.161
2021 FS	CHC	MLB	33	2	2	0	57	0	50	46	5	4.2	8.5	47	51.4%	.292

Comparables: Chuck McElroy, Ryan Tepera, Bryan Shaw

Notable predictions made by inventor Ray Kurzweil included the demise of the Soviet Union because of new technologies; that computers could beat the best human chess players by the year 2000; and the invention of text-to-speech devices for the blind. Big deal; we'd like to see Kurzweil predict what's to come from Jeffress during any given season. The veteran right-hander went from All-Star and dependable late-inning arm to being released by the Brewers in the span of a year, so naturally he became the Cubs' best reliever in 2020, supplanting Craig Kimbrel as closer and hocus-pocusing his way through the shortened season with just four earned runs crossing the plate. That success came despite an arsenal change (more splitters, fewer fastballs) that saw his whiff rate sink to unthinkable depths while his walk rate skyrocketed. Relievers are weird, and relievers in a 60-game season are even weirder, so even Kurzweil would struggle to figure out what Jeffress is likeliest to do in 2021.

YEAR	TEAM	LVL	AGE	WHIP	ERA	DRA-	WARP	MPH	FB%	WHF	CSP
2018	MIL	MLB	30	0.99	1.29	58	2.0	97.4	53.2%	31.0%	
2019	MIL	MLB	31	1.37	5.02	98	0.3	95.8	64.3%	20.8%	
2020	CHC	MLB	32	0.94	1.54	101	0.2	94.7	41.3%	24.6%	
2021 FS	CHC	MLB	33	1.39	4.14	94	0.4	96.0	55.0%	24.9%	46.6%

Jeremy Jeffress, continued

Pitch Shape vs LHH

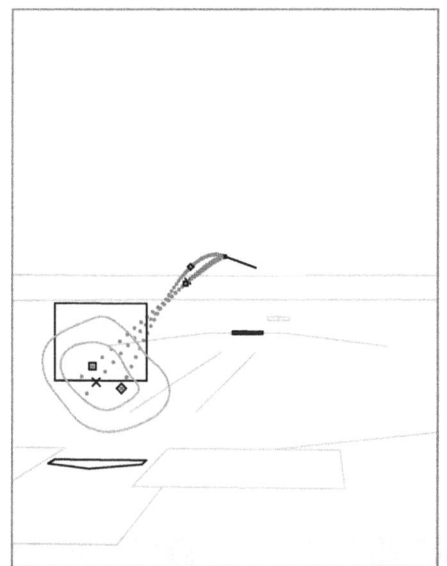

Pitch Shape vs RHH

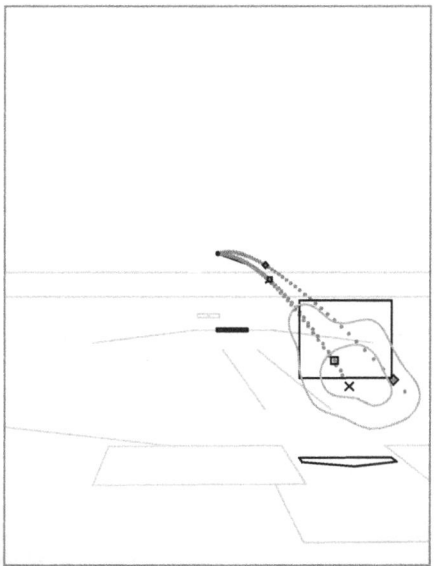

Type	Frequency	Velocity	H Movement	V Movement
● Fastball	10.8%	93.5 [103]	-6.8 [99]	-14.9 [101]
□ Sinker	29.9%	93.4 [105]	-14.4 [90]	-20.1 [101]
✕ Splitter	33.1%	89 [117]	-9.9 [93]	-27.7 [106]
◇ Curveball	24.7%	80.6 [108]	7.4 [99]	-42 [114]

Chicago Cubs 2021

Craig Kimbrel RHP
Born: 05/28/88 Age: 33 Bats: R Throws: R
Height: 6'0" Weight: 215 Origin: Round 3, 2008 Draft (#96 overall)

YEAR	TEAM	LVL	AGE	W	L	SV	G	GS	IP	H	HR	BB/9	K/9	K	GB%	BABIP
2018	BOS	MLB	30	5	1	42	63	0	62^1	31	7	4.5	13.9	96	28.8%	.218
2019	CHC	MLB	31	0	4	13	23	0	20^2	21	9	5.2	13.1	30	28.8%	.279
2020	CHC	MLB	32	0	1	2	18	0	15^1	10	2	7.0	16.4	28	33.3%	.320
2021 FS	CHC	MLB	33	2	2	28	57	0	50	36	7	4.5	13.2	73	33.8%	.283
2021 DC	CHC	MLB	33	2	2	28	45	0	48.3	35	7	4.5	13.2	71	33.8%	.283

Comparables: Kenley Jansen, Dellin Betances, Billy Wagner

In Kimbrel's first appearance of the season, he faced six batters, walked four and got one out. In his second appearance, he faced five batters and allowed two home runs. In his third appearance, he faced three batters and two of them reached base. In his fourth appearance, he pitched an inning and allowed a run. Kimbrel was actually quite good after that, posting a 1.54 ERA after being removed from the closer's role, and he went the entire month of September without issuing a walk. Kimbrel is unlikely to return to his dominant peak as he enters his mid-30s, but there's still a talented reliever in there. After two uneven, abbreviated seasons in Chicago, maybe a normal one will finally allow us to see it.

YEAR	TEAM	LVL	AGE	WHIP	ERA	DRA-	WARP	MPH	FB%	WHF	CSP
2018	BOS	MLB	30	0.99	2.74	57	1.7	98.9	64.6%	40.0%	
2019	CHC	MLB	31	1.60	6.53	124	-0.2	97.8	66.6%	32.8%	
2020	CHC	MLB	32	1.43	5.28	80	0.3	98.5	62.3%	35.4%	
2021 FS	CHC	MLB	33	1.22	3.41	80	0.8	98.5	64.4%	36.5%	41.6%
2021 DC	CHC	MLB	33	1.22	3.41	80	0.8	98.5	64.4%	36.5%	41.6%

Craig Kimbrel, continued

Pitch Shape vs LHH

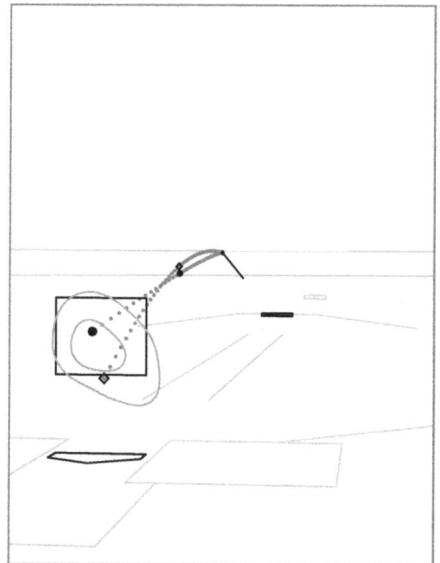

Pitch Shape vs RHH

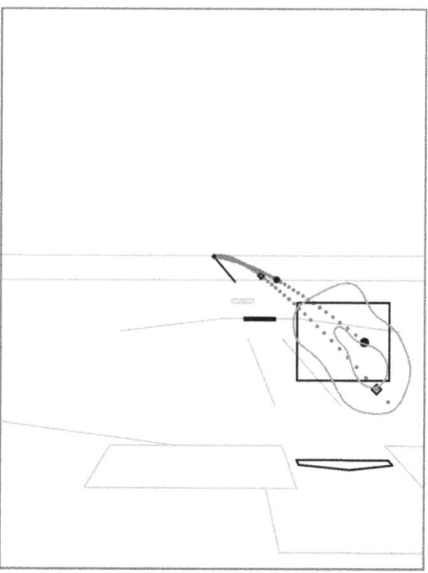

Type	Frequency	Velocity	H Movement	V Movement
● Fastball	61.9%	97.1 [114]	-9.5 [87]	-13.4 [105]
◇ Curveball	37.4%	86.2 [129]	9.8 [109]	-39 [121]

Chicago Cubs 2021

Alec Mills   RHP
Born: 11/30/91   Age: 29   Bats: R   Throws: R
Height: 6'4"   Weight: 205   Origin: Round 22, 2012 Draft (#673 overall)

YEAR	TEAM	LVL	AGE	W	L	SV	G	GS	IP	H	HR	BB/9	K/9	K	GB%	BABIP
2018	IOW	AAA	26	5	12	0	23	23	124²	121	10	3.0	7.8	108	39.1%	.307
2018	CHC	MLB	26	0	1	0	7	2	18	11	1	3.5	11.5	23	51.2%	.250
2019	IOW	AAA	27	6	4	0	19	18	104	116	17	2.6	8.3	96	38.6%	.332
2019	CHC	MLB	27	1	0	1	9	4	36	31	5	2.8	10.5	42	48.9%	.299
2020	CHC	MLB	28	5	5	0	11	11	62¹	53	13	2.7	6.6	46	47.6%	.233
2021 FS	CHC	MLB	29	9	8	0	26	26	150	142	21	3.0	8.1	134	44.7%	.288
2021 DC	CHC	MLB	29	8	7	0	25	24	131	124	18	3.0	8.1	117	44.7%	.288

Comparables: Chris Stratton, Luke Farrell, Austin Voth

In the annals of unlikely no-hitters, Mills' feat—accomplished September 13th against the Brewers—doesn't quite rank with the likes of Philip Humber or Bud Smith. He's certainly no Bobo Holloman, either, and there is no evidence that he was on LSD. But Mills' feat was, undeniably, unlikely. The soft-tossing right-hander did it with a fastball that ticks in four miles per hour slower than the league-average heater. He did it after being a college walk-on. He did it as a former 22nd-round pick. And he did it after three years spent as Quad-A roster filler. Unexpected no-hitters don't always launch grand careers—see some of the names above—but the most important part of Mills' year is that he established himself as a legitimate back-of-the-rotation starter who can get out big-league hitters with his deception and his contact-management skills. Perhaps, given everything else we knew about Mills entering the year, that's the most unlikely part of his season. (Nah, it's still the no-no.)

YEAR	TEAM	LVL	AGE	WHIP	ERA	DRA-	WARP	MPH	FB%	WHF	CSP
2018	IOW	AAA	26	1.30	4.84	80	2.5				
2018	CHC	MLB	26	1.00	4.00	54	0.6	92.2	58.9%	27.6%	
2019	IOW	AAA	27	1.40	5.11	90	2.3				
2019	CHC	MLB	27	1.17	2.75	75	0.7	91.4	54.2%	28.1%	
2020	CHC	MLB	28	1.16	4.48	117	0.0	91.6	58.9%	18.0%	
2021 FS	CHC	MLB	29	1.29	3.97	92	2.1	91.6	57.7%	21.3%	46.1%
2021 DC	CHC	MLB	29	1.29	3.97	92	1.7	91.6	57.7%	21.3%	46.1%

Alec Mills, continued

Pitch Shape vs LHH

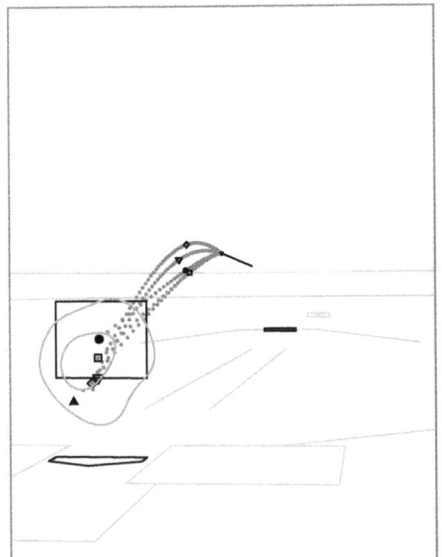

Pitch Shape vs RHH

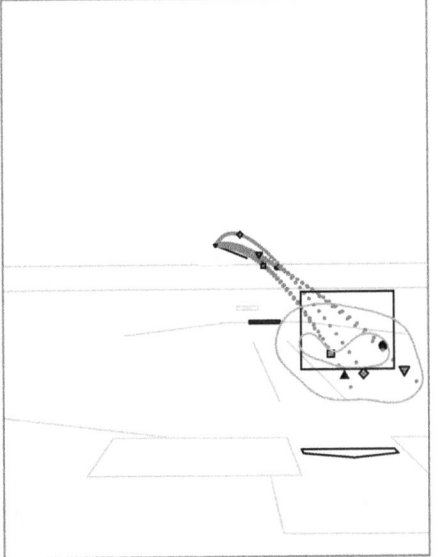

Type	Frequency	Velocity	H Movement	V Movement
● Fastball	25.5%	90 [92]	-8.4 [92]	-17.8 [93]
□ Sinker	33.4%	90.2 [89]	-14.4 [90]	-23.5 [90]
▲ Changeup	16.0%	81 [84]	-13.6 [90]	-34.1 [82]
▽ Slider	10.1%	77.7 [72]	14.7 [136]	-43 [73]
◇ Curveball	15.0%	66.8 [54]	11.4 [116]	-64.9 [63]

Adam Morgan   LHP

Born: 02/27/90   Age: 31   Bats: L   Throws: L
Height: 6'1"   Weight: 200   Origin: Round 3, 2011 Draft (#120 overall)

YEAR	TEAM	LVL	AGE	W	L	SV	G	GS	IP	H	HR	BB/9	K/9	K	GB%	BABIP
2018	PHI	MLB	28	0	2	1	67	0	49^1	49	5	4.0	9.1	50	51.8%	.324
2019	PHI	MLB	29	3	3	0	40	0	29^2	20	4	3.0	8.8	29	41.0%	.216
2020	PHI	MLB	30	0	1	0	17	0	13	14	3	4.2	11.1	16	47.2%	.333
2021 FS	CHC	MLB	31	2	2	0	57	0	50	44	7	3.2	9.3	51	42.2%	.284

Comparables: Matt Andriese, Neil Ramírez, Mike Montgomery

The Phillies planned for Morgan to be one of their impact arms in the pen this year, given a solid 2019 cut short by a flexor strain. The injury took some bite off his fastball, so he started relying on it less and his off-speed stuff more. That led to pumping his slider in there with career-high frequency in 2020, keeping lefties hitting only .200 against him. Unfortunately, the approach left him naked against right-handers, who battered his weak changeup and sent liners whizzing past him to the tune of a .364 BAA. It was an unfortunate year to pick to become a LOOGY. Morgan had elbow surgery on that pesky flexor tendon at the end of the season, in hopes of being back to 100 percent in 2021, but there's no surgical procedure to keep him from having to face righties.

YEAR	TEAM	LVL	AGE	WHIP	ERA	DRA-	WARP	MPH	FB%	WHF	CSP
2018	PHI	MLB	28	1.44	3.83	96	0.4	95.7	34.7%	28.7%	
2019	PHI	MLB	29	1.01	3.94	87	0.4	93.8	28.1%	33.3%	
2020	PHI	MLB	30	1.54	5.54	80	0.3	93.5	33.8%	33.3%	
2021 FS	CHC	MLB	31	1.25	3.75	89	0.5	94.4	31.9%	31.7%	46.9%

Adam Morgan, continued

Pitch Shape vs LHH

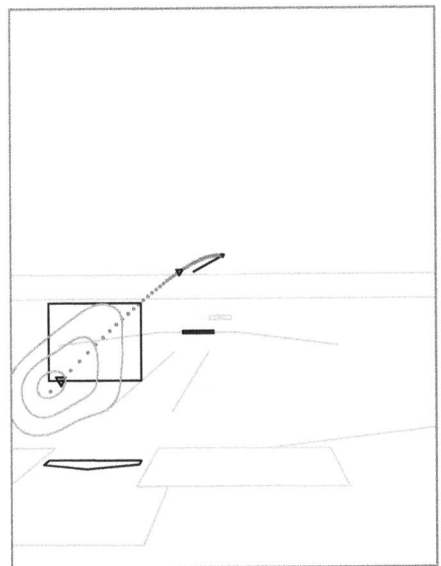

Pitch Shape vs RHH

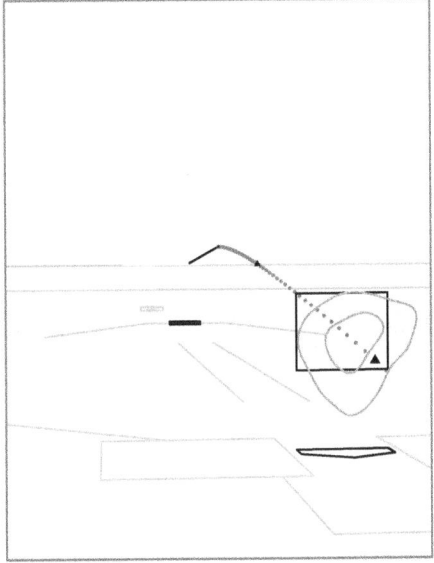

Type	Frequency	Velocity	H Movement	V Movement
● Fastball	20.1%	91.8 [98]	10.7 [81]	-15.7 [99]
□ Sinker	13.7%	91.5 [95]	16.8 [73]	-21.8 [96]
▲ Changeup	16.4%	83.7 [94]	13.1 [93]	-27.8 [99]
▽ Slider	45.7%	81.7 [90]	-7.4 [108]	-32.9 [102]
◇ Curveball	4.1%	77.3 [95]	-8.4 [103]	-49.6 [97]

Chicago Cubs 2021

Colin Rea RHP
Born: 07/01/90 Age: 31 Bats: R Throws: R
Height: 6'5" Weight: 235 Origin: Round 12, 2011 Draft (#383 overall)

YEAR	TEAM	LVL	AGE	W	L	SV	G	GS	IP	H	HR	BB/9	K/9	K	GB%	BABIP
2018	SA	AA	27	0	3	0	6	6	24	32	3	4.9	7.9	21	39.0%	.367
2018	ELP	AAA	27	3	2	0	12	9	51^1	58	11	4.0	8.6	49	43.4%	.336
2019	IOW	AAA	28	14	4	0	26	26	148	142	17	3.6	7.3	120	44.8%	.294
2020	CHC	MLB	29	1	1	0	9	2	14	15	3	1.3	6.4	10	44.0%	.255
2021 FS	*CHC*	*MLB*	*30*	*2*	*3*	*0*	*57*	*0*	*50*	*51*	*8*	*3.6*	*7.3*	*40*	*43.0%*	*.288*

Comparables: Jordan Lyles, Kendall Graveman, Chris Stratton

Rea saw his fair share of mop-up work in the final month of the season. He's still going to be known as the person whose injury situation forced the Padres to trade Luis Castillo back to the Marlins just three days after acquiring him.

YEAR	TEAM	LVL	AGE	WHIP	ERA	DRA-	WARP	MPH	FB%	WHF	CSP
2018	SA	AA	27	1.88	7.12	81	0.4				
2018	ELP	AAA	27	1.58	5.08	103	0.4				
2019	IOW	AAA	28	1.36	3.95	83	3.8				
2020	CHC	MLB	29	1.21	5.79	111	0.0	95.0	51.4%	17.4%	
2021 FS	*CHC*	*MLB*	*30*	*1.42*	*4.86*	*109*	*0.0*	*95.0*	*51.4%*	*17.4%*	*51.7%*

Colin Rea, continued

Pitch Shape vs LHH	Pitch Shape vs RHH
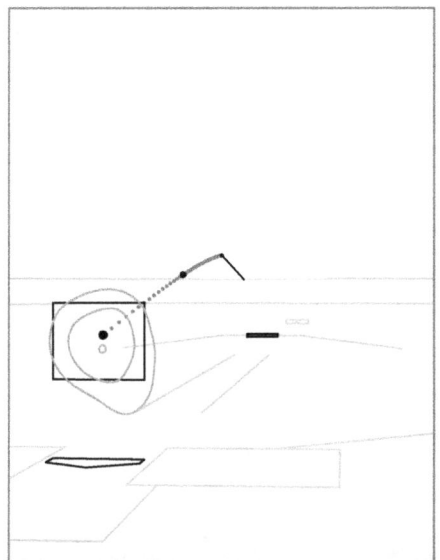	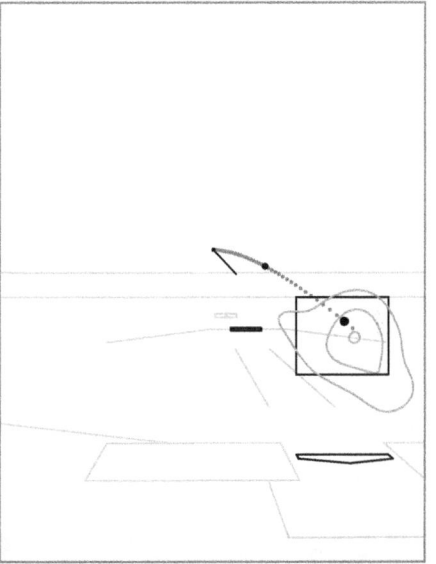

Type	Frequency	Velocity	H Movement	V Movement
● Fastball	36.6%	93.3 [102]	-6.6 [100]	-15.1 [100]
□ Sinker	14.8%	92.6 [101]	-11.4 [112]	-19.3 [104]
+ Cutter	17.7%	87.2 [93]	3.1 [108]	-26.3 [92]
▲ Changeup	11.5%	85.4 [101]	-12.8 [94]	-25.3 [106]
◇ Curveball	19.3%	80.6 [108]	7.1 [98]	-45.8 [106]

Kyle Ryan LHP

Born: 09/25/91 Age: 29 Bats: L Throws: L
Height: 6'5" Weight: 215 Origin: Round 12, 2010 Draft (#373 overall)

YEAR	TEAM	LVL	AGE	W	L	SV	G	GS	IP	H	HR	BB/9	K/9	K	GB%	BABIP
2018	IOW	AAA	26	1	2	0	22	8	66	48	9	2.5	8.3	61	58.9%	.236
2019	CHC	MLB	27	4	2	0	73	0	61	55	5	4.3	8.6	58	56.7%	.301
2020	CHC	MLB	28	1	0	1	18	0	15^2	16	5	3.4	6.3	11	49.0%	.250
2021 FS	CHC	MLB	29	2	2	0	57	0	50	47	6	3.7	7.9	44	51.8%	.290
2021 DC	CHC	MLB	29	2	2	0	51	0	36.3	34	4	3.7	7.9	32	51.8%	.290

Comparables: Luke Jackson, Drew VerHagen, A.J. Cole

There have been 21 players in major-league history with the surname Ryan. Nolan, of course, leads them all with 157.9 career WARP. More recently, there was Brendan and B.J. Before that, there was a John, a Johnny, three Mikes and three Jacks, none of whom inspired the Amazon original series. In the 1800s, there was even a Cyclone Ryan, who was from Capperwhite, Ireland, and who played in 12 total games for the New York Metropolitans and Boston Beaneaters. This Ryan, Kyle, is the first of his name to ever grace a major-league field. While he'll never reach the stature of the all-timer Nolan, nor finish with the career wealth of Brendan or B.J., he should continue to find work as a low-leverage sinkerballer capable of overcoming the platoon advantage.

YEAR	TEAM	LVL	AGE	WHIP	ERA	DRA-	WARP	MPH	FB%	WHF	CSP
2018	IOW	AAA	26	1.00	2.86	71	1.5				
2019	CHC	MLB	27	1.38	3.54	82	0.9	91.1	46.7%	23.6%	
2020	CHC	MLB	28	1.40	5.17	126	-0.1	90.5	51.9%	16.7%	
2021 FS	CHC	MLB	29	1.36	4.09	94	0.4	90.9	48.1%	21.7%	46.9%
2021 DC	CHC	MLB	29	1.36	4.09	94	0.3	90.9	48.1%	21.7%	46.9%

Kyle Ryan, continued

Pitch Shape vs LHH

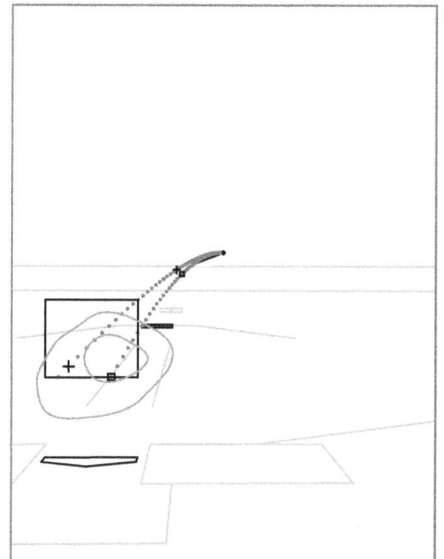

Pitch Shape vs RHH

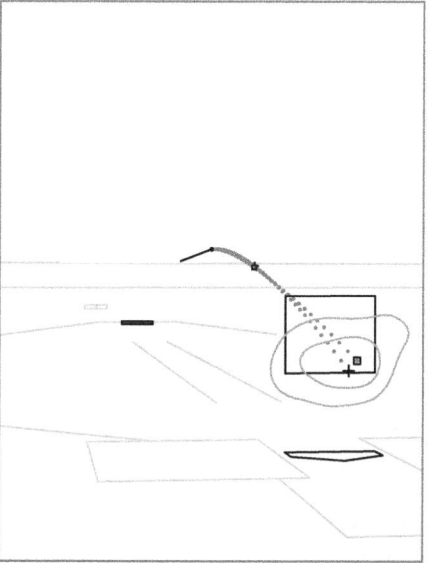

Type	Frequency	Velocity	H Movement	V Movement
● Fastball	17.2%	89.1 [89]	3 [118]	-20.8 [84]
☐ Sinker	34.7%	87.7 [76]	7.5 [141]	-28.1 [75]
+ Cutter	39.6%	85.2 [80]	-3.3 [109]	-29.2 [80]
▽ Slider	8.6%	78.2 [74]	-9.1 [115]	-44 [70]

Ryan Tepera RHP

Born: 11/03/87 Age: 33 Bats: R Throws: R
Height: 6'1" Weight: 195 Origin: Round 19, 2009 Draft (#580 overall)

YEAR	TEAM	LVL	AGE	W	L	SV	G	GS	IP	H	HR	BB/9	K/9	K	GB%	BABIP
2018	TOR	MLB	30	5	5	7	68	0	64^2	55	9	3.3	9.5	68	43.7%	.291
2019	TOR	MLB	31	0	2	0	23	1	21^2	20	5	3.3	5.8	14	42.0%	.238
2020	CHC	MLB	32	0	1	0	21	0	20^2	17	2	5.2	13.5	31	40.0%	.349
2021 FS	CHC	MLB	33	2	2	0	57	0	50	43	7	4.1	10.0	55	42.0%	.286

Comparables: Ryan Brasier, Jeremy Jeffress, Luis García

Matthew Lewis, Dev Patel, Ryan Tepera. What are memorable glow-ups, Alex? Tepera spent five years in Toronto as a mostly anonymous middle reliever who was pretty solid in the run-prevention department, but lacking the type of stuff that would allow you to trust him in high-leverage spots. In his first year in Chicago, he upped his strikeout rate, not just incrementally, but to more than four strikeouts per nine more than any other season in his career. His whiff rate was in the 99th percentile in the majors, generating swinging strikes on nearly half of his pitches. The reason? An uptick in the usage of his cutter, which looks like his fastball coming out but features a serious late dip and about a six-mph difference. The walk rate went up along with the strikeouts, which prevented Tepera from truly entering "elite reliever" territory, but like Neville Longbottom or the Slumdog Millionaire, he went from "oh yeah, that guy" to someone who earned a MVP vote (accidentally or not, it still counts).

YEAR	TEAM	LVL	AGE	WHIP	ERA	DRA-	WARP	MPH	FB%	WHF	CSP
2018	TOR	MLB	30	1.22	3.62	109	0.0	96.7	61.3%	30.6%	
2019	TOR	MLB	31	1.29	4.98	122	-0.1	95.0	57.1%	26.3%	
2020	CHC	MLB	32	1.40	3.92	80	0.4	95.4	46.1%	44.0%	
2021 FS	CHC	MLB	33	1.34	4.17	94	0.4	95.8	54.3%	34.8%	39.9%

Ryan Tepera, continued

Pitch Shape vs LHH

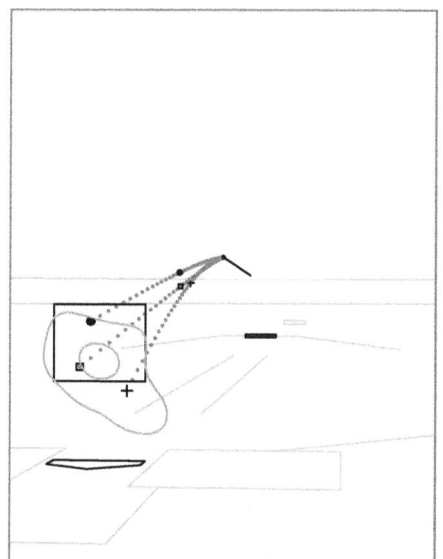

Pitch Shape vs RHH

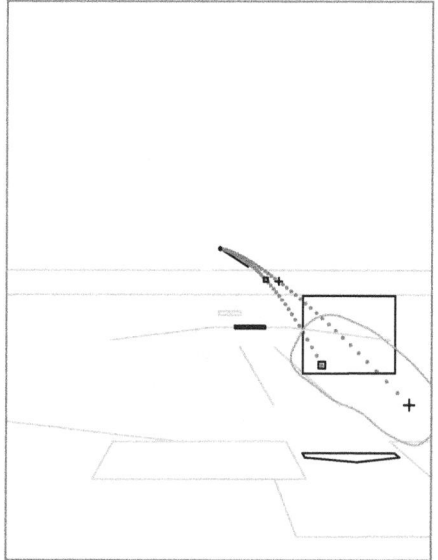

Type	Frequency	Velocity	H Movement	V Movement
● Fastball	17.1%	93.9 [104]	-7.4 [96]	-12.8 [107]
☐ Sinker	29.0%	94.2 [109]	-13.7 [95]	-16.7 [112]
+ Cutter	43.6%	87.9 [97]	2.9 [106]	-26.3 [92]
× Splitter	5.1%	85.2 [100]	-7.6 [101]	-28.6 [103]
▽ Slider	5.1%	82.4 [93]	4.2 [96]	-37.9 [88]

Duane Underwood Jr. RHP

Born: 07/20/94   Age: 26   Bats: R   Throws: R
Height: 6'2"   Weight: 210   Origin: Round 2, 2012 Draft (#67 overall)

YEAR	TEAM	LVL	AGE	W	L	SV	G	GS	IP	H	HR	BB/9	K/9	K	GB%	BABIP
2018	IOW	AAA	23	4	10	0	27	20	119^1	127	8	2.8	7.9	105	41.2%	.337
2018	CHC	MLB	23	0	1	0	1	1	4	2	1	6.8	6.8	3	50.0%	.111
2019	IOW	AAA	24	3	7	0	33	10	81^2	84	8	4.5	10.5	95	45.7%	.349
2019	CHC	MLB	24	0	0	0	12	0	11^2	13	2	2.3	10.0	13	50.0%	.344
2020	CHC	MLB	25	1	0	0	17	0	20^2	25	5	2.6	11.8	27	38.9%	.408
2021 FS	CHC	MLB	26	2	2	0	57	0	50	45	7	4.1	9.5	52	42.7%	.291
2021 DC	CHC	MLB	26	2	2	0	51	0	48.3	44	7	4.1	9.5	51	42.7%	.291

Comparables: Alex Reyes, Lucas Sims, Ricardo Pinto

The Cubs have been waiting for Underwood to become a quality part of their bullpen for so long that it's easy to forget that they were once waiting for him to become a quality part of their rotation. He finally saw regular major-league action in 2020, and while he was limited to low-leverage work, he showed signs of having some staying power despite his unsightly ERA. Underwood began relying more on his changeup than ever before and saw a career-best whiff rate with it. A lot of strikeouts and few walks is a recipe for success for any pitcher, but Underwood allowed too much contact to be counted on for high-leverage work. Still, there's something to be said for becoming a legitimate big-league relief option—like that it's more than we'd seen from him in the past, and it's reason to keep an eye on him in 2021.

YEAR	TEAM	LVL	AGE	WHIP	ERA	DRA-	WARP	MPH	FB%	WHF	CSP
2018	IOW	AAA	23	1.37	4.53	78	2.5				
2018	CHC	MLB	23	1.25	2.25	178	-0.1	94.5	53.2%	12.1%	
2019	IOW	AAA	24	1.53	5.07	79	2.1				
2019	CHC	MLB	24	1.37	5.40	75	0.2	96.7	59.5%	27.3%	
2020	CHC	MLB	25	1.50	5.66	89	0.3	96.6	46.3%	36.4%	
2021 FS	CHC	MLB	26	1.37	4.29	97	0.3	96.5	50.3%	32.6%	44.0%
2021 DC	CHC	MLB	26	1.37	4.29	97	0.4	96.5	50.3%	32.6%	44.0%

Duane Underwood Jr., continued

Pitch Shape vs LHH

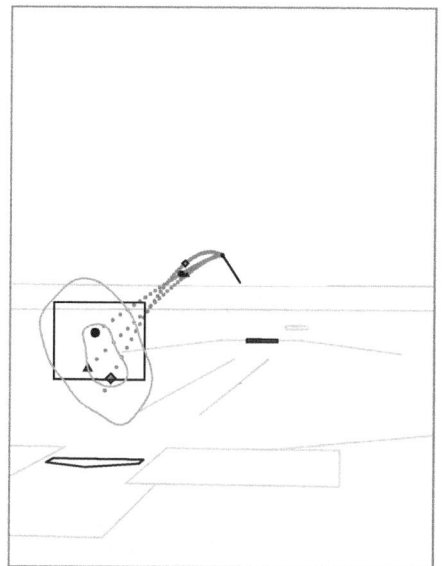

Pitch Shape vs RHH

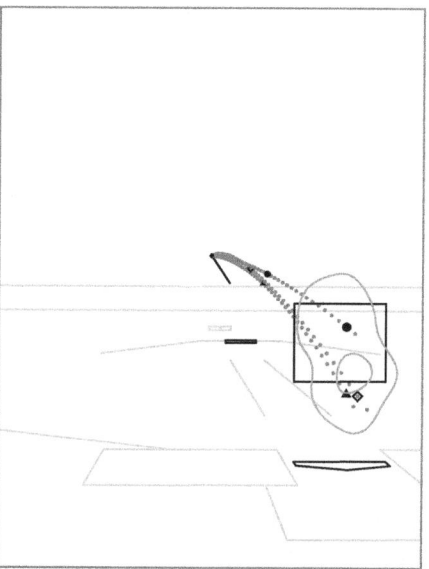

Type	Frequency	Velocity	H Movement	V Movement
● Fastball	44.0%	94.6 [107]	-7.1 [98]	-14.2 [103]
▲ Changeup	28.6%	87.3 [108]	-12.2 [97]	-26.7 [102]
◇ Curveball	24.5%	81.7 [112]	6.5 [96]	-44.8 [108]

Rowan Wick RHP

Born: 11/09/92 Age: 28 Bats: L Throws: R
Height: 6'3" Weight: 234 Origin: Round 9, 2012 Draft (#300 overall)

YEAR	TEAM	LVL	AGE	W	L	SV	G	GS	IP	H	HR	BB/9	K/9	K	GB%	BABIP
2018	SA	AA	25	2	4	5	29	0	31¹	22	0	6.0	12.1	42	56.3%	.314
2018	ELP	AAA	25	2	0	9	20	0	22²	16	3	4.0	8.7	22	45.9%	.224
2018	SD	MLB	25	0	1	0	10	0	8¹	13	1	1.1	7.6	7	36.7%	.414
2019	IOW	AAA	26	1	0	6	27	0	35	25	3	2.3	11.3	44	48.8%	.272
2019	CHC	MLB	26	2	0	2	31	0	33¹	22	0	4.3	9.4	35	53.5%	.259
2020	CHC	MLB	27	0	1	4	19	0	17¹	18	1	3.1	10.4	20	39.6%	.362
2021 FS	CHC	MLB	28	2	2	12	57	0	50	43	6	3.8	9.9	55	44.3%	.289
2021 DC	CHC	MLB	28	2	2	12	51	0	48.3	42	6	3.8	9.9	53	44.3%	.289

Comparables: Dan Altavilla, Phil Maton, Jonathan Holder

On August 22, Wick entered the Cubs' game against the White Sox in the seventh inning with his team trailing 3-2. He walked Yasmani Grandal on five pitches, and then got ahead 0-2 on José Abreu. On the fourth pitch of that plate appearance, Abreu deposited a hanging curve into the left-field bleachers. That the home run came amid a stretch of six homers in three days by Abreu made it, perhaps, inevitable. But it was notable for Wick in that it was his first allowed in 45 ⅔ innings, a stretch that included 47 games dating back to Sept. 7, 2019, when, as a San Diego Padre, he allowed a home run to the Reds' Scott Schebler. Sure, Abreu lit up Wick, but the righty has helped turn out the lights on opponents ever since the Cubs acquired him at a small cost.

YEAR	TEAM	LVL	AGE	WHIP	ERA	DRA-	WARP	MPH	FB%	WHF	CSP
2018	SA	AA	25	1.37	3.16	62	0.7				
2018	ELP	AAA	25	1.15	1.99	103	0.1				
2018	SD	MLB	25	1.68	6.48	91	0.1	96.2	87.2%	20.3%	
2019	IOW	AAA	26	0.97	1.80	37	1.5				
2019	CHC	MLB	26	1.14	2.43	78	0.5	97.3	68.0%	26.1%	
2020	CHC	MLB	27	1.38	3.12	87	0.3	96.3	65.2%	25.9%	
2021 FS	CHC	MLB	28	1.29	3.75	87	0.6	96.9	68.0%	25.7%	49.0%
2021 DC	CHC	MLB	28	1.29	3.75	87	0.6	96.9	68.0%	25.7%	49.0%

Rowan Wick, continued

Pitch Shape vs LHH

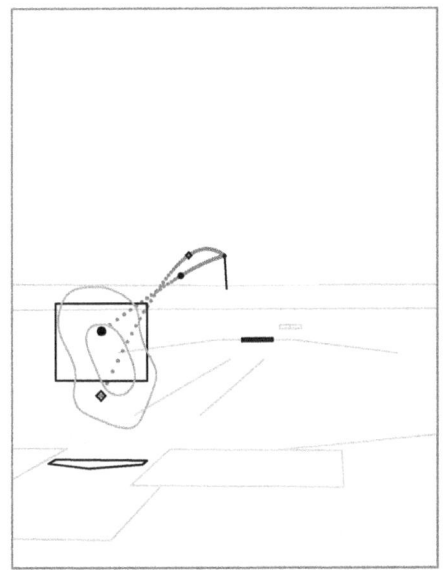

Pitch Shape vs RHH

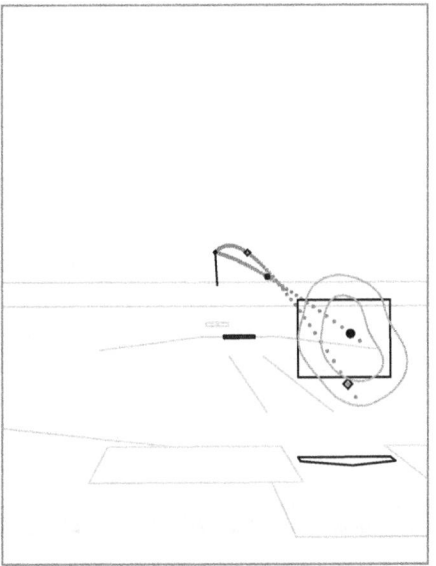

Type	Frequency	Velocity	H Movement	V Movement
● Fastball	50.6%	95.1 [108]	-0.8 [128]	-10.7 [113]
+ Cutter	12.7%	92 [123]	4.1 [114]	-19.4 [119]
◇ Curveball	33.8%	76.9 [93]	6 [93]	-58.4 [78]

Trevor Williams RHP
Born: 04/25/92 Age: 29 Bats: R Throws: R
Height: 6'3" Weight: 235 Origin: Round 2, 2013 Draft (#44 overall)

YEAR	TEAM	LVL	AGE	W	L	SV	G	GS	IP	H	HR	BB/9	K/9	K	GB%	BABIP
2018	PIT	MLB	26	14	10	0	31	31	170^2	146	15	2.9	6.6	126	40.5%	.265
2019	PIT	MLB	27	7	9	0	26	26	145^2	162	27	2.7	7.0	113	36.9%	.308
2020	PIT	MLB	28	2	8	0	11	11	55^1	66	15	3.4	8.0	49	43.3%	.315
2021 FS	CHC	MLB	29	2	2	0	57	0	50	48	7	3.1	7.6	42	42.1%	.286
2021 DC	CHC	MLB	29	6	6	0	6	21	101	99	15	3.1	7.6	85	42.1%	.286

Comparables: José Ureña, Kevin Gausman, Mike Foltynewicz

After drastically altering his pitch mix early in the season, almost halving his use of the fastball, by late September his usage had crept back up, and with it a league-leading number of homers surrendered. A peek at his xBA/xSLG indicates he's been unlucky with his breaking pitches, but it's been an undeniably bumpy road for Williams in the Steel City. Always open and unflinchingly honest, Williams is the first to admit the 2020 season wore at him on and off the mound; unfortunately for him, the pitching-rich Pirates didn't need to keep him around to figure things out. Instead, they thanked him for the memes and designated him for assignment.

YEAR	TEAM	LVL	AGE	WHIP	ERA	DRA-	WARP	MPH	FB%	WHF	CSP
2018	PIT	MLB	26	1.18	3.11	95	2.0	93.2	69.4%	18.9%	
2019	PIT	MLB	27	1.41	5.38	117	0.1	93.6	66.7%	22.4%	
2020	PIT	MLB	28	1.57	6.18	130	-0.4	93.3	51.1%	24.3%	
2021 FS	CHC	MLB	29	1.32	4.28	98	0.3	93.4	62.8%	22.1%	45.1%
2021 DC	CHC	MLB	29	1.32	4.28	98	1.1	93.4	62.8%	22.1%	45.1%

Trevor Williams, continued

Pitch Shape vs LHH

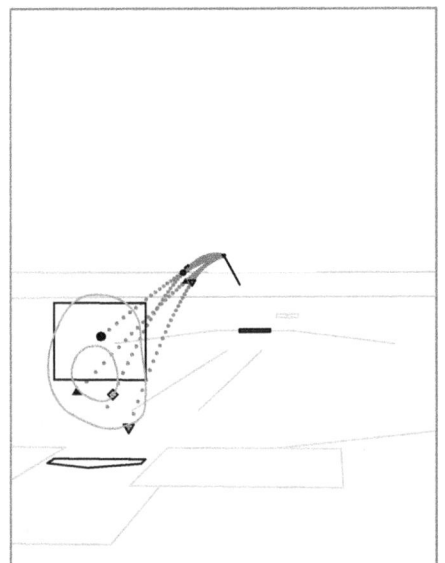

Pitch Shape vs RHH

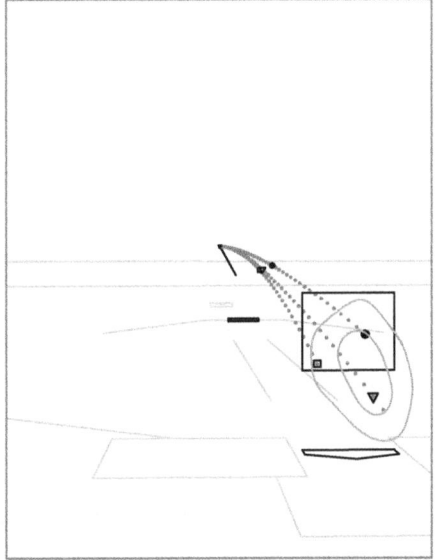

Type	Frequency	Velocity	H Movement	V Movement
● Fastball	42.6%	91.8 [97]	-3.2 [117]	-17 [95]
☐ Sinker	8.6%	89.8 [87]	-11.8 [110]	-23.7 [90]
▲ Changeup	15.1%	85.3 [101]	-11.9 [99]	-26.4 [103]
▽ Slider	27.2%	82.8 [95]	6.4 [104]	-35.8 [94]
◇ Curveball	6.5%	78 [97]	8 [102]	-43.1 [112]

Dan Winkler RHP

Born: 02/02/90   Age: 31   Bats: R   Throws: R
Height: 6'3"   Weight: 205   Origin: Round 20, 2011 Draft (#618 overall)

YEAR	TEAM	LVL	AGE	W	L	SV	G	GS	IP	H	HR	BB/9	K/9	K	GB%	BABIP
2018	ATL	MLB	28	4	0	2	69	0	60^1	52	3	3.0	10.3	69	39.8%	.312
2019	SAC	AAA	29	0	1	0	12	0	14	6	1	3.2	5.8	9	56.8%	.139
2019	GWN	AAA	29	0	1	2	18	0	16^2	16	1	9.7	10.8	20	41.3%	.333
2019	ATL	MLB	29	3	1	0	27	0	21^2	18	5	4.6	9.1	22	30.5%	.241
2020	CHC	MLB	30	0	0	0	18	0	18^1	11	3	5.4	8.8	18	41.3%	.190
2021 FS	CHC	MLB	31	2	2	0	57	0	50	43	7	4.8	9.3	51	40.0%	.279
2021 DC	CHC	MLB	31	2	2	0	51	0	48.3	42	7	4.8	9.3	50	40.0%	.279

Comparables: Mychal Givens, Raisel Iglesias, Pedro Báez

Winkler entered the ninth inning of Game 1 of the Cubs' Wild Card Series against the Marlins, faced three batters, retired them all and struck out two. That was a fairly standard appearance for him in 2020—not so much the result, but the fact that he came into a game in which the result was all but decided. Ah, right, we forgot to mention that the Marlins were leading 5-1 when Winkler entered. Those are the kinds of situations he found himself pitching in all year long. To wit: of the 76 batters Winkler faced last season, 42 were classified as "low-leverage" plate appearances. Good enough for a spot in the bullpen, just not good enough to trust with the game on the line. It's not a glamorous job, but hey, it pays the bills.

YEAR	TEAM	LVL	AGE	WHIP	ERA	DRA-	WARP	MPH	FB%	WHF	CSP
2018	ATL	MLB	28	1.19	3.43	78	1.0	94.8	33.9%	28.5%	
2019	SAC	AAA	29	0.79	0.64	45	0.5				
2019	GWN	AAA	29	2.04	4.86	118	0.1				
2019	ATL	MLB	29	1.34	4.98	127	-0.2	94.1	33.9%	33.5%	
2020	CHC	MLB	30	1.20	2.95	110	0.1	94.7	32.4%	27.6%	
2021 FS	CHC	MLB	31	1.42	4.49	100	0.3	94.6	33.4%	29.5%	42.2%
2021 DC	CHC	MLB	31	1.42	4.49	100	0.2	94.6	33.4%	29.5%	42.2%

Dan Winkler, continued

Pitch Shape vs LHH

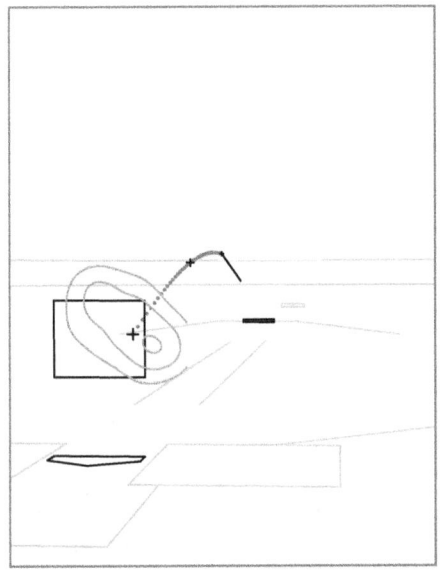

Pitch Shape vs RHH

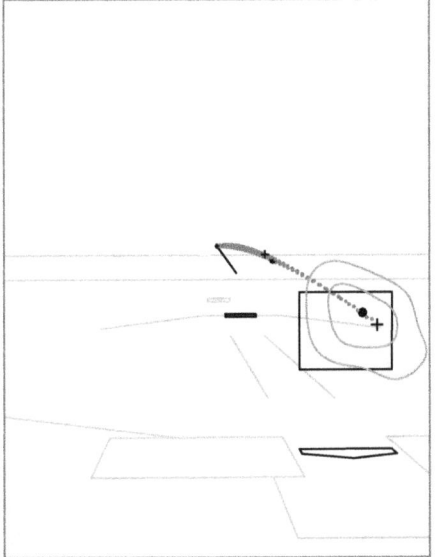

Type	Frequency	Velocity	H Movement	V Movement
● Fastball	22.7%	93 [101]	-4.1 [112]	-15.6 [99]
☐ Sinker	9.7%	92.5 [100]	-10.8 [117]	-18.5 [106]
+ Cutter	54.8%	88.2 [99]	4.1 [114]	-25.4 [95]
▽ Slider	11.7%	82.5 [93]	8.2 [111]	-36.9 [91]

PLAYER COMMENTS WITHOUT GRAPHS

Sergio Alcántara SS
Born: 07/10/96   Age: 24   Bats: S   Throws: R
Height: 5'9"   Weight: 151   Origin: International Free Agent, 2012

YEAR	TEAM	LVL	AGE	PA	R	2B	3B	HR	RBI	BB	K	SB	CS	AVG/OBP/SLG
2018	ERI	AA	21	494	53	18	3	1	37	42	95	8	5	.271/.335/.333
2019	ERI	AA	22	378	46	10	0	2	26	48	71	7	6	.247/.346/.296
2020	DET	MLB	23	23	2	0	1	1	1	2	4	0	0	.143/.217/.381
2021 FS	CHC	MLB	24	600	68	25	2	9	59	50	140	3	3	.236/.304/.343
2021 DC	CHC	MLB	24	60	6	2	0	0	5	5	14	0	0	.236/.304/.343

Comparables: Jack Reinheimer, Tony Giarratano, Cristhian Adames

The scrawny Alcántara seared the major leagues last year, as he started off with a home run in his debut game, a triple in his second, and probably should have halted the season there. The corrugated cardboard lumber he swings will keep him from earning anything more than a smattering of playing time: The thing about having the bat knocked out of your hands is that it at least insinuates the ability to make contact. He and teammate Harold Castro are the two lightest players in baseball in the last 10 years (151 pounds). Stack one on the other's shoulders and you've got quite the second baseman.

YEAR	TEAM	LVL	AGE	PA	DRC+	BABIP	BRR	FRAA	WARP
2018	ERI	AA	21	494	88	.342	-2.5	SS(93): -0.6, 2B(20): -0.3	0.3
2019	ERI	AA	22	378	100	.308	0.1	SS(73): 4.4, 2B(29): 1.8	2.2
2020	DET	MLB	23	23	88	.125	0.0	2B(6): -0.9, 3B(6): -0.4	-0.1
2021 FS	CHC	MLB	24	600	79	.302	-0.3	SS 1, 2B -1	0.1
2021 DC	CHC	MLB	24	60	79	.302	0.0	SS 0, 2B 0	0.0

Miguel Amaya C
Born: 03/09/99 Age: 22 Bats: R Throws: R
Height: 6'2" Weight: 230 Origin: International Free Agent, 2015

YEAR	TEAM	LVL	AGE	PA	R	2B	3B	HR	RBI	BB	K	SB	CS	AVG/OBP/SLG
2018	SB	LO-A	19	479	54	21	2	12	52	50	91	1	0	.256/.349/.403
2019	MB	HI-A	20	410	50	24	0	11	57	54	69	2	0	.235/.351/.402
2021 FS	CHC	MLB	22	600	67	25	1	15	68	37	156	2	1	.217/.278/.355
2021 DC	CHC	MLB	22	67	7	2	0	1	7	4	17	0	0	.217/.278/.355

Comparables: Austin Hedges, Alejandro Kirk, Luis Campusano

"A collection of 50s and 55s" was used to describe Amaya in last year's Top 101. That's not super exciting, but it's more than okay when you're talking about a lower-minors catcher with a legitimate shot at sticking behind the plate. During his summer at the Cubs' alternate training site, the team worked on getting Amaya to tap into some of his pull-side power, which he's previously shown in BP but has yet to get into games. If Amaya starts to pair in-game power with his above-average plate discipline, if he continues making good contact and working all fields and if he makes the expected strides defensively…all right, that's a lot of ifs, but the point is that Amaya has a chance to be really good, and his potential seems well within his reach.

YEAR	TEAM	LVL	AGE	PA	DRC+	BABIP	BRR	FRAA	WARP
2018	SB	LO-A	19	479	117	.298	0.6	C(95): 2.5, 1B(9): -0.7	2.5
2019	MB	HI-A	20	410	124	.259	-3.6	C(91): 2.8	2.7
2021 FS	CHC	MLB	22	600	71	.274	-0.6	C 1, 1B 0	0.2
2021 DC	CHC	MLB	22	67	71	.274	-0.1	C 0	0.0

Brennen Davis CF
Born: 11/02/99 Age: 21 Bats: R Throws: R
Height: 6'4" Weight: 175 Origin: Round 2, 2018 Draft (#62 overall)

YEAR	TEAM	LVL	AGE	PA	R	2B	3B	HR	RBI	BB	K	SB	CS	AVG/OBP/SLG
2018	CUBR	ROK	18	72	9	2	0	0	3	10	12	6	1	.298/.431/.333
2019	SB	LO-A	19	204	33	9	3	8	30	18	38	4	1	.305/.381/.525
2021 FS	CHC	MLB	21	600	56	23	3	14	60	41	169	6	3	.225/.289/.357

Comparables: Jesse Winker, Christian Yelich, Alen Hanson

Davis has spent enough time in South Bend, Indiana to be mistaken for a Notre Dame student. After breaking out there in the Midwest League a year ago, Davis was forced to go back in 2020, working out at the Cubs' alternate site instead of what was expected to be a promotion to Double-A Tennessee. The Cubs valued his development enough to have him in their player pool, and why wouldn't they? At maturation, he could be their starting center fielder while featuring five average or better tools.

Chicago Cubs 2021

YEAR	TEAM	LVL	AGE	PA	DRC+	BABIP	BRR	FRAA	WARP
2018	CUBR	ROK	18	72		.370			
2019	SB	LO-A	19	204	154	.346	-0.6	LF(23): -1.2, CF(23): -2.1, RF(2): 0.7	1.4
2021 FS	CHC	MLB	21	600	78	.298	0.2	CF 5, LF 1	0.7

Daniel Descalso 2B
Born: 10/19/86   Age: 34   Bats: L   Throws: R
Height: 5'10"   Weight: 190   Origin: Round 3, 2007 Draft (#112 overall)

YEAR	TEAM	LVL	AGE	PA	R	2B	3B	HR	RBI	BB	K	SB	CS	AVG/OBP/SLG
2018	ARI	MLB	31	423	54	22	4	13	57	64	110	0	1	.238/.353/.436
2019	IOW	AAA	32	33	5	0	0	2	4	5	8	0	0	.148/.303/.370
2019	CHC	MLB	32	194	20	5	1	2	15	23	57	2	1	.173/.271/.250
2021 FS	CHC	MLB	34	600	62	24	3	15	63	74	164	4	2	.212/.316/.363

Comparables: Tony Graffanino, Dick Green, Damian Jackson

In November 2018, the Cubs traded utility infielder Tommy La Stella to the Angels for a PTBNL. A month later, they replaced him with Descalso. La Stella became an All-Star, Descalso very much did not.

YEAR	TEAM	LVL	AGE	PA	DRC+	BABIP	BRR	FRAA	WARP
2018	ARI	MLB	31	423	105	.300	-0.7	2B(52): 3.2, 3B(37): -0.8, 1B(11): -0.0	1.8
2019	IOW	AAA	32	33	74	.118	-0.3	2B(5): -0.0, 3B(4): -0.6	-0.1
2019	CHC	MLB	32	194	59	.245	-0.5	2B(45): 2.1, 3B(3): -0.1, 1B(1): -0.0	-0.2
2021 FS	CHC	MLB	34	600	87	.279	-0.1	2B 3, 3B -2	0.6

Ed Howard SS
Born: 08/06/01   Age: 19   Bats: R   Throws: R
Height: 6'2"   Weight: 185   Origin: Round 1, 2020 Draft (#16 overall)

Howard, a product of the White Sox ACE program (which aims to help inner-city Chicago youth develop skills and find opportunities on and off the field), wound up on the other side of town when the Cubs nabbed him 16th overall in last June's draft. As a prep infielder from a cold-weather state, Howard wasn't able to showcase himself much before the pandemic shut down baseball across the globe, but the Cubs obviously believe in his advanced glove and projectable bat. Howard is, almost by default, one of the organization's most important developmental projects as they transition from one era to the next.

Dixon Machado SS

Born: 02/22/92 Age: 29 Bats: R Throws: R
Height: 6'1" Weight: 190 Origin: International Free Agent, 2008

YEAR	TEAM	LVL	AGE	PA	R	2B	3B	HR	RBI	BB	K	SB	CS	AVG/OBP/SLG
2018	TOL	AAA	26	171	19	5	0	1	8	18	28	4	2	.224/.321/.279
2018	DET	MLB	26	233	20	13	1	1	21	14	41	1	1	.206/.263/.290
2019	IOW	AAA	27	393	53	19	1	17	65	54	79	0	2	.261/.371/.480
2020	LOT	KBO	28	560	79	31	1	12	67	54	60	15	1	.280/.356/.422
2021 FS	CHC	MLB	29	600	60	27	1	14	63	53	128	1	1	.236/.313/.376

Comparables: Ryan Jackson, Mike Rouse, Edwin Maysonet

Limited by the rules to just one position player—at least until 2021—most KBO teams opt to sign a slugger to anchor the middle of their order. Lotte took a different tack, signing the glove-first Machado and hoping that his 2019 Triple-A numbers would translate to climes without such a juicy baseball. Good move. The former Tiger managed a better than league average line at the plate, but shone particularly brightly in the field. In a circuit where even the most routine grounders to short can't be taken for granted, the 28-year-old dazzled with a collection of highlight plays and provided the league's sturdiest defense at the six. By far the biggest difference in the quality of play between the KBO and the big leagues shows up on defense, and it's thus a little surprising that more teams haven't signed their own Dixon Machado. Perhaps his success in 2020 will spark a trend.

YEAR	TEAM	LVL	AGE	PA	DRC+	BABIP	BRR	FRAA	WARP
2018	TOL	AAA	26	171	82	.271	0.0	SS(25): -0.2, 2B(16): 3.2	0.4
2018	DET	MLB	26	233	70	.249	1.5	2B(64): 0.8	0.1
2019	IOW	AAA	27	393	103	.295	0.0	SS(74): 4.0, 2B(16): 1.1, 1B(7): 0.4	2.2
2020	LOT	KBO	28	560					
2021 FS	CHC	MLB	29	600	90	.284	-0.8	SS 1, 2B 2	1.3

Josh Phegley C

Born: 02/12/88 Age: 33 Bats: R Throws: R
Height: 5'10" Weight: 225 Origin: Round 1, 2009 Draft (#38 overall)

YEAR	TEAM	LVL	AGE	PA	R	2B	3B	HR	RBI	BB	K	SB	CS	AVG/OBP/SLG
2018	NAS	AAA	30	139	12	6	3	3	18	15	31	0	0	.235/.331/.412
2018	OAK	MLB	30	102	13	7	0	2	15	6	27	0	0	.204/.255/.344
2019	OAK	MLB	31	342	44	18	0	12	62	15	63	0	1	.239/.282/.411
2020	CHC	MLB	32	18	4	0	0	1	2	1	3	0	0	.062/.167/.250
2021 FS	CHC	MLB	33	600	60	26	1	17	66	40	138	2	1	.222/.289/.373

Comparables: Mark Parent, Rod Barajas, Vance Wilson

Chicago Cubs 2021

Phegley made the Cubs' Opening Day roster thanks to the expanded bench, but he was relegated to the alternate site as soon as the rosters were contracted. He's probably best deployed as a third catcher heading forward, though it shouldn't surprise anyone if he gets another run or two as a primary backup.

YEAR	TEAM	P. COUNT	FRM RUNS	BLK RUNS	THRW RUNS	TOT RUNS
2018	OAK	3985	-0.9	-1.5	0.0	-2.3
2018	NAS	2495	2.4	-0.2	0.3	2.5
2019	OAK	13331	-7.1	-5.5	1.0	-11.6
2020	CHC	267	-0.1	0.0	0.0	-0.1
2021	CHC	16650	-8.7	-1.2	-0.5	-10.4
2021	CHC	16650	-8.7	-6.5	-0.5	-15.7

YEAR	TEAM	LVL	AGE	PA	DRC+	BABIP	BRR	FRAA	WARP
2018	NAS	AAA	30	139	101	.287	-0.1	C(19): 2.8	0.6
2018	OAK	MLB	30	102	75	.258	-0.1	C(39): -1.3	0.1
2019	OAK	MLB	31	342	90	.258	-3.0	C(106): -14.3	-0.3
2020	CHC	MLB	32	18	93	.000	0.1	C(4): -0.0	0.0
2021 FS	CHC	MLB	33	600	81	.265	-0.7	C -16	-0.7

Heliot Ramos   CF
Born: 09/07/99   Age: 21   Bats: R   Throws: R
Height: 6'0"   Weight: 188   Origin: Round 1, 2017 Draft (#19 overall)

YEAR	TEAM	LVL	AGE	PA	R	2B	3B	HR	RBI	BB	K	SB	CS	AVG/OBP/SLG
2018	AUG	LO-A	18	535	61	24	8	11	52	35	136	8	7	.245/.313/.396
2019	SJ	HI-A	19	338	51	18	0	13	40	32	85	6	7	.306/.385/.500
2019	RIC	AA	19	106	13	6	1	3	15	10	33	2	3	.242/.321/.421
2021 FS	CHC	MLB	21	600	65	21	6	15	65	37	217	5	4	.214/.273/.361
2021 DC	CHC	MLB	21	33	3	1	0	0	3	2	11	0	0	.214/.273/.361

Comparables: Jo Adell, Anthony Gose, Cristian Pache

A rough 2019 introduction to Double-A and the rapid ascendancy of Marco Luciano pushed Ramos into the shadows a bit. He's still there, the bat is still great, but the profile is now more corner-outfield than center. Trimming the swing-and-miss should be the last challenge for Ramos to clear before leveling up to the majors.

YEAR	TEAM	LVL	AGE	PA	DRC+	BABIP	BRR	FRAA	WARP
2018	AUG	LO-A	18	535	106	.319	1.8	CF(113): -4.5	0.7
2019	SJ	HI-A	19	338	142	.385	0.1	CF(71): -5.1	1.7
2019	RIC	AA	19	106	120	.339	-1.6	CF(19): -1.5	0.2
2021 FS	CHC	MLB	21	600	74	.320	0.7	CF 0	0.0
2021 DC	CHC	MLB	21	33	74	.320	0.0	RF 0	0.0

Cole Roederer CF

Born: 09/24/99   Age: 21   Bats: L   Throws: L
Height: 6'0"   Weight: 175   Origin: Round 2, 2018 Draft (#77 overall)

YEAR	TEAM	LVL	AGE	PA	R	2B	3B	HR	RBI	BB	K	SB	CS	AVG/OBP/SLG
2018	CUBR	ROK	18	161	30	4	4	5	24	18	37	13	4	.275/.354/.465
2019	SB	LO-A	19	448	45	19	4	9	60	52	112	16	5	.224/.319/.365
2021 FS	CHC	MLB	21	600	47	21	4	11	53	39	205	12	5	.193/.250/.306

Comparables: Trent Grisham, Slade Heathcott, Joe Benson

Roederer was drafted with the compensation pick the Cubs received when Jake Arrieta signed with the Phillies. He struggled in his first full-season assignment in the Midwest League, but he has plenty of time for the bat to come around. In the meantime, he has at least looked like he can stick in center.

YEAR	TEAM	LVL	AGE	PA	DRC+	BABIP	BRR	FRAA	WARP
2018	CUBR	ROK	18	161		.337			
2019	SB	LO-A	19	448	91	.285	1.6	CF(95): 3.3, LF(9): -0.7, RF(3): -0.4	1.4
2021 FS	CHC	MLB	21	600	50	.283	1.4	CF 12, LF 0	-0.6

Addison Russell 2B

Born: 01/23/94   Age: 27   Bats: R   Throws: R
Height: 6'0"   Weight: 200   Origin: Round 1, 2012 Draft (#11 overall)

YEAR	TEAM	LVL	AGE	PA	R	2B	3B	HR	RBI	BB	K	SB	CS	AVG/OBP/SLG
2018	CHC	MLB	24	465	52	21	1	5	38	40	99	4	0	.250/.317/.340
2019	IOW	AAA	25	119	25	6	0	7	26	14	25	1	2	.281/.387/.562
2019	CHC	MLB	25	241	25	4	1	9	23	20	58	2	0	.237/.308/.391
2020	KIW	KBO	26	271	22	14	0	2	31	22	37	2	0	.254/.317/.336
2021 FS	CHC	MLB	27	600	68	23	2	21	73	56	154	3	2	.236/.319/.412

Comparables: Jose Valentin, Jed Lowrie, Dansby Swanson

My, how the mighty have fallen.

YEAR	TEAM	LVL	AGE	PA	DRC+	BABIP	BRR	FRAA	WARP
2018	CHC	MLB	24	465	80	.314	-0.8	SS(129): 1.2	1.0
2019	IOW	AAA	25	119	113	.294	-0.1	SS(18): 0.4, 2B(7): 1.7	0.8
2019	CHC	MLB	25	241	83	.280	0.0	2B(63): 3.4, SS(21): -0.2	0.7
2020	KIW	KBO	26	271					
2021 FS	CHC	MLB	27	600	99	.292	-0.4	SS 1, 2B 4	2.3

Chicago Cubs 2021

Chase Strumpf 2B

Born: 03/08/98   Age: 23   Bats: R   Throws: R
Height: 6'1"   Weight: 191   Origin: Round 2, 2019 Draft (#64 overall)

YEAR	TEAM	LVL	AGE	PA	R	2B	3B	HR	RBI	BB	K	SB	CS	AVG/OBP/SLG
2019	CUBR	ROK	21	32	5	3	0	0	1	7	7	0	0	.182/.406/.318
2019	EUG	SS	21	111	17	8	0	2	14	15	28	2	0	.292/.405/.449
2019	SB	LO-A	21	28	3	1	0	1	2	1	7	0	0	.125/.214/.292
2021 FS	CHC	MLB	23	600	51	22	2	12	54	42	205	2	1	.194/.264/.309

Strumpf has an advanced approach that will need to carry him since nothing else grades out as above-average, including every part of his surname between the "S" and the "F."

YEAR	TEAM	LVL	AGE	PA	DRC+	BABIP	BRR	FRAA	WARP
2019	CUBR	ROK	21	32		.250			
2019	EUG	SS	21	111	151	.387	-1.3	2B(24): -3.4	0.3
2019	SB	LO-A	21	28	50	.118	0.0	2B(6): 0.2	-0.1
2021 FS	CHC	MLB	23	600	59	.285	-0.5	2B -3	-1.7

Cory Abbott RHP

Born: 09/20/95   Age: 25   Bats: R   Throws: R
Height: 6'2"   Weight: 220   Origin: Round 2, 2017 Draft (#67 overall)

YEAR	TEAM	LVL	AGE	W	L	SV	G	GS	IP	H	HR	BB/9	K/9	K	GB%	BABIP
2018	SB	LO-A	22	4	1	0	9	9	47^1	35	5	2.5	10.8	57	38.6%	.275
2018	MB	HI-A	22	4	5	0	13	13	67^2	59	3	3.5	9.8	74	44.4%	.316
2019	TNS	AA	23	8	8	0	26	26	146^2	112	15	3.2	10.2	166	37.5%	.270
2021 FS	CHC	MLB	25	2	2	0	57	0	50	45	8	4.4	9.2	51	36.9%	.284
2021 DC	CHC	MLB	25	0	0	0	4	3	12.7	11	2	4.4	9.2	13	36.9%	.284

Comparables: Ramón Rosso, Matt Hall, Nabil Crismatt

Abbott has moved slowly since being a second-round pick in 2017, but he spent the season at the alternate site and was added to the 40-man roster ahead of the Rule 5 draft. He should be in the mix for a starting shot at some point this year.

YEAR	TEAM	LVL	AGE	WHIP	ERA	DRA-	WARP	MPH	FB%	WHF	CSP
2018	SB	LO-A	22	1.01	2.47	61	1.3				
2018	MB	HI-A	22	1.26	2.53	106	0.3				
2019	TNS	AA	23	1.12	3.01	86	1.4				
2021 FS	CHC	MLB	25	1.40	4.48	104	0.1				
2021 DC	CHC	MLB	25	1.40	4.48	104	0.1				

Joe Biagini   RHP

Born: 05/29/90   Age: 31   Bats: R   Throws: R
Height: 6'5"   Weight: 235   Origin: Round 26, 2011 Draft (#807 overall)

YEAR	TEAM	LVL	AGE	W	L	SV	G	GS	IP	H	HR	BB/9	K/9	K	GB%	BABIP
2018	BUF	AAA	28	0	3	0	4	4	21^2	19	1	3.3	5.4	13	45.1%	.257
2018	TOR	MLB	28	4	7	0	50	4	72	96	14	3.0	6.6	53	47.3%	.355
2019	HOU	MLB	29	0	1	0	13	0	14^2	21	6	5.5	6.1	10	50.0%	.341
2019	TOR	MLB	29	3	1	1	50	0	50	50	8	3.1	9.0	50	44.4%	.311
2020	HOU	MLB	30	0	0	0	4	0	4^1	10	1	8.3	8.3	4	47.4%	.500
2021 FS	CHC	MLB	31	2	2	0	57	0	50	50	8	3.5	7.7	42	46.5%	.297

Comparables: Erasmo Ramírez, Jacob Barnes, Felix Peña

Here's one mystery the Astros couldn't solve. The brief clues available on what attempts were made to rejuvenate Biagini's career hinted at an against-the-grain emphasis on the sinker, with a curveball-cutter secondary mix and the four-seam fastball exterminated altogether. It did nothing to arrest the decline Biagini suffered after arriving in Houston. He was bumped off the roster after the season ended, and picked up by the Cubs.

YEAR	TEAM	LVL	AGE	WHIP	ERA	DRA-	WARP	MPH	FB%	WHF	CSP
2018	BUF	AAA	28	1.25	4.57	88	0.3				
2018	TOR	MLB	28	1.67	6.00	127	-0.6	96.6	60.8%	20.6%	
2019	HOU	MLB	29	2.05	7.36	241	-1.0	94.8	57.8%	21.6%	
2019	TOR	MLB	29	1.34	3.78	97	0.3	95.2	48.5%	30.5%	
2020	HOU	MLB	30	3.23	20.77	92	0.1	94.8	63.6%	28.3%	
2021 FS	CHC	MLB	31	1.40	4.57	102	0.2	95.5	55.2%	25.9%	43.8%

Rex Brothers   LHP

Born: 12/18/87   Age: 33   Bats: L   Throws: L
Height: 6'0"   Weight: 205   Origin: Round 1, 2009 Draft (#34 overall)

YEAR	TEAM	LVL	AGE	W	L	SV	G	GS	IP	H	HR	BB/9	K/9	K	GB%	BABIP
2018	MIS	AA	30	3	1	0	11	0	13^1	7	1	7.4	12.8	19	46.7%	.207
2018	GWN	AAA	30	2	4	1	32	0	27^1	26	1	10.9	12.2	37	43.5%	.391
2018	ATL	MLB	30	0	0	0	1	0	0	0	0			0		
2019	SWB	AAA	31	0	3	0	34	0	45^2	37	6	7.1	16.0	81	38.2%	.378
2020	CHC	MLB	32	0	0	0	3	0	3^1	2	2	8.1	21.6	8	25.0%	.000
2021 FS	CHC	MLB	33	2	2	0	57	0	50	39	6	7.3	13.2	73	40.9%	.312

Comparables: Anthony Bass, Brad Boxberger, Brandon Morrow

The Brothers Grimm is an underrated adventure fantasy film released in 2005 by Terry Gillam of *Monty Python* and *Brazil* fame. Rex Brothers is an up-and-down reliever whose major-league story seems likely to end soon, if not happily.

Chicago Cubs 2021

YEAR	TEAM	LVL	AGE	WHIP	ERA	DRA-	WARP	MPH	FB%	WHF	CSP
2018	MIS	AA	30	1.35	4.05	64	0.3				
2018	GWN	AAA	30	2.16	7.24	96	0.1				
2018	ATL	MLB	30					98.0	91.7%	0.0%	
2019	SWB	AAA	31	1.60	4.93	82	1.0				
2020	CHC	MLB	32	1.50	8.10	80	0.1	97.2	53.3%	48.5%	
2021 FS	CHC	MLB	33	1.61	4.87	104	0.1	97.2	55.3%	46.0%	33.1%

Burl Carraway   LHP
Born: 05/27/99   Age: 22   Bats: L   Throws: L
Height: 6'0"   Weight: 173   Origin: Round 2, 2020 Draft (#51 overall)

With a name that sounds like someone cast in a John Huston film, Carraway features a rising fastball with elite velo and a 12-6 curveball that figures to induce its share of whiffs. Whether or not his other pitches develop like the Cubs hoped when they drafted him in the second round will determine whether he's an A-list celebrity or some forgettable face relegated to the background.

Ryan Jensen   RHP
Born: 11/23/97   Age: 23   Bats: R   Throws: R
Height: 6'0"   Weight: 180   Origin: Round 1, 2019 Draft (#27 overall)

YEAR	TEAM	LVL	AGE	W	L	SV	G	GS	IP	H	HR	BB/9	K/9	K	GB%	BABIP
2019	EUG	SS	21	0	0	0	6	6	12	7	0	10.5	14.2	19	68.2%	.318
2021 FS	CHC	MLB	23	2	3	0	57	0	50	47	8	8.5	9.1	50	44.9%	.287

Comparables: Dillon Tate, Spencer Turnbull, Humberto Mejía

The Cubs' first-round pick in 2019, Jensen started for only one year in college and, as a result, carries significant risk. That he wasn't included at the team's alternate site means we won't know exactly what the Cubs have here for a while longer.

YEAR	TEAM	LVL	AGE	WHIP	ERA	DRA-	WARP	MPH	FB%	WHF	CSP
2019	EUG	SS	21	1.75	2.25	141	-0.2				
2021 FS	CHC	MLB	23	1.89	6.66	135	-0.7				

Dillon Maples   RHP
Born: 05/09/92   Age: 29   Bats: R   Throws: R
Height: 6'2"   Weight: 230   Origin: Round 14, 2011 Draft (#429 overall)

YEAR	TEAM	LVL	AGE	W	L	SV	G	GS	IP	H	HR	BB/9	K/9	K	GB%	BABIP
2018	IOW	AAA	26	2	3	10	41	0	38^2	22	1	9.1	17.5	75	57.4%	.350
2018	CHC	MLB	26	1	0	0	9	0	5^1	7	2	8.4	15.2	9	30.8%	.455
2019	IOW	AAA	27	4	4	7	38	0	43	21	1	7.5	16.5	79	62.7%	.303
2019	CHC	MLB	27	1	0	0	14	0	11^2	6	2	7.7	13.9	18	68.2%	.200
2020	CHC	MLB	28	0	0	0	2	0	1	1	0	36.0	9.0	1	25.0%	.250
2021 FS	CHC	MLB	29	2	3	0	57	0	50	39	5	7.7	13.3	73	52.4%	.314
2021 DC	CHC	MLB	29	1	1	0	22	0	12	9	1	7.7	13.3	17	52.4%	.314

Comparables: Giovanny Gallegos, Carl Edwards Jr., Dominic Leone

The abbreviated Dillon Maples Experience was much the same as the full-season version: a clean inning with a strikeout on a trademark slider, followed by a four-walk outing in which he failed to retire a batter. Only Maples could raise a career walk rate already approaching 20 percent.

YEAR	TEAM	LVL	AGE	WHIP	ERA	DRA-	WARP	MPH	FB%	WHF	CSP
2018	IOW	AAA	26	1.58	2.79	10	2.2				
2018	CHC	MLB	26	2.25	11.81	108	0.0	98.5	23.9%	20.5%	
2019	IOW	AAA	27	1.33	3.77	27	2.0				
2019	CHC	MLB	27	1.37	5.40	82	0.2	98.3	33.3%	44.2%	
2020	CHC	MLB	28	5.00	18.00	119	0.0	98.1	37.5%	60.0%	
2021 FS	CHC	MLB	29	1.64	4.97	105	0.1	98.3	32.2%	42.2%	43.6%
2021 DC	CHC	MLB	29	1.64	4.97	105	0.0	98.3	32.2%	42.2%	43.6%

Brailyn Marquez LHP

Born: 01/30/99 Age: 22 Bats: L Throws: L
Height: 6'4" Weight: 185 Origin: International Free Agent, 2015

YEAR	TEAM	LVL	AGE	W	L	SV	G	GS	IP	H	HR	BB/9	K/9	K	GB%	BABIP
2018	EUG	SS	19	1	4	0	10	10	47²	46	5	2.6	9.8	52	50.8%	.333
2018	SB	LO-A	19	0	0	0	2	2	7	7	0	2.6	9.0	7	33.3%	.333
2019	SB	LO-A	20	5	4	0	17	17	77¹	64	4	5.0	11.9	102	50.8%	.337
2019	MB	HI-A	20	4	1	0	5	5	26¹	21	1	2.4	8.9	26	44.4%	.282
2020	CHC	MLB	21	0	0	0	1	0	0²	2	0	40.5	13.5	1	33.3%	.667
2021 FS	CHC	MLB	22	9	9	0	26	26	150	143	22	4.9	8.9	148	44.1%	.295
2021 DC	CHC	MLB	22	4	3	0	32	4	46.3	44	7	4.9	8.9	46	44.1%	.295

Comparables: Huascar Ynoa, Julio Teheran, Luis Severino

Walk, walk, wild pitch, RBI groundout, strikeout, walk, wild pitch, double. The Cubs promoted Marquez ahead of their season finale, giving the young left-hander what amounted to a playoff audition. He entered in the eighth inning against the White Sox in a game the Cubs were leading 10-1, and that was the sequence of events that followed. Suffice it to say it didn't work, and he instead wound up watching the Cubs' two playoff games from the comfort of the taxi squad. That Marquez was even considered for such a role is evidence of the promise the lefty showed while spending the season working at the team's alternate training site. He remains one of the most talented near-ready arms in the minor leagues, even if his career 67.50 ERA might hurt to look at until that next opportunity comes around.

YEAR	TEAM	LVL	AGE	WHIP	ERA	DRA-	WARP	MPH	FB%	WHF	CSP
2018	EUG	SS	19	1.26	3.21	272	-4.3				
2018	SB	LO-A	19	1.29	2.57	75	0.1				
2019	SB	LO-A	20	1.38	3.61	108	-0.1				
2019	MB	HI-A	20	1.06	1.71	81	0.3				
2020	CHC	MLB	21	7.50	67.50	133	0.0	99.5	48.5%	36.4%	
2021 FS	CHC	MLB	22	1.50	4.96	109	0.6	99.5	48.5%	36.4%	36.8%
2021 DC	CHC	MLB	22	1.50	4.96	109	0.0	99.5	48.5%	36.4%	36.8%

Justin Steele LHP
Born: 07/11/95 Age: 25 Bats: L Throws: L
Height: 6'2" Weight: 205 Origin: Round 5, 2014 Draft (#139 overall)

YEAR	TEAM	LVL	AGE	W	L	SV	G	GS	IP	H	HR	BB/9	K/9	K	GB%	BABIP
2018	CUBB	ROK	22	0	0	0	5	5	18^1	9	1	2.0	13.3	27	40.5%	.229
2018	MB	HI-A	22	2	1	0	4	4	18^1	12	0	2.9	9.3	19	41.3%	.261
2018	TNS	AA	22	0	1	0	2	2	10	8	1	2.7	6.3	7	22.6%	.241
2019	TNS	AA	23	0	6	0	11	11	38^2	45	3	4.7	9.8	42	39.3%	.412
2021 FS	CHC	MLB	25	9	9	0	26	26	150	140	21	4.9	8.6	143	40.0%	.288
2021 DC	CHC	MLB	25	3	2	0	30	3	32.7	30	4	4.9	8.6	31	40.0%	.288

Comparables: Albert Abreu, Bernardo Flores Jr., Hector Perez

Steele spent three days on the Cubs' active roster without making an appearance. He's got a long way to go before his name starts showing up in Google search results over the director of such cinematic masterpieces as *Death and Cremation*, *Gutshot Straight* and, of course, *Sergeant X*.

YEAR	TEAM	LVL	AGE	WHIP	ERA	DRA-	WARP	MPH	FB%	WHF	CSP
2018	CUBB	ROK	22	0.71	1.47						
2018	MB	HI-A	22	0.98	2.45	85	0.3				
2018	TNS	AA	22	1.10	3.60	79	0.2				
2019	TNS	AA	23	1.68	5.59	137	-0.8				
2021 FS	CHC	MLB	25	1.48	4.82	108	0.8				
2021 DC	CHC	MLB	25	1.48	4.82	108	0.1				

Brad Wieck LHP

Born: 10/14/91 Age: 29 Bats: L Throws: L
Height: 6'8" Weight: 257 Origin: Round 7, 2014 Draft (#205 overall)

YEAR	TEAM	LVL	AGE	W	L	SV	G	GS	IP	H	HR	BB/9	K/9	K	GB%	BABIP
2018	SA	AA	26	1	2	10	27	0	28	20	1	2.6	11.6	36	29.0%	.279
2018	ELP	AAA	26	3	0	2	17	0	18^1	16	2	4.4	16.7	34	42.1%	.400
2018	SD	MLB	26	0	0	0	5	0	7	3	1	0.0	12.9	10	28.6%	.154
2019	IOW	AAA	27	1	0	0	6	0	5^2	4	0	4.8	17.5	11	22.2%	.444
2019	ELP	AAA	27	1	1	2	14	0	17^2	16	5	3.1	17.3	34	29.4%	.379
2019	SD	MLB	27	0	1	0	30	0	24^2	26	7	3.3	11.3	31	33.3%	.306
2019	CHC	MLB	27	2	1	0	14	0	10	2	1	3.6	16.2	18	21.4%	.077
2020	CHC	MLB	28	0	0	0	1	0	1	1	1	9.0	18.0	2	0.0%	.000
2021 FS	CHC	MLB	29	2	2	0	57	0	50	38	7	3.9	12.5	69	35.0%	.288
2021 DC	CHC	MLB	29	1	1	0	34	0	24	18	3	3.9	12.5	33	35.0%	.288

Comparables: Kyle Finnegan, Phillips Valdez, Daniel Stumpf

Wieck pitched in the Cubs' season opener against the Brewers, and then was shut down with a hamstring strain and leg injury that eventually cost him the rest of the season. The tall lefty will now have to generate anew the momentum he had this time last year.

YEAR	TEAM	LVL	AGE	WHIP	ERA	DRA-	WARP	MPH	FB%	WHF	CSP
2018	SA	AA	26	1.00	1.93	53	0.8				
2018	ELP	AAA	26	1.36	3.44	40	0.7				
2018	SD	MLB	26	0.43	1.29	59	0.2	93.4	64.5%	30.0%	
2019	IOW	AAA	27	1.24	1.59	115	0.0				
2019	ELP	AAA	27	1.25	6.11	58	0.6				
2019	SD	MLB	27	1.42	6.57	113	-0.1	95.3	79.9%	24.3%	
2019	CHC	MLB	27	0.60	3.60	15	0.5	95.0	71.1%	37.8%	
2020	CHC	MLB	28	2.00	18.00	85	0.0	92.0	70.0%	33.3%	
2021 FS	CHC	MLB	29	1.20	3.41	81	0.8	95.0	76.2%	28.1%	47.9%
2021 DC	CHC	MLB	29	1.20	3.41	81	0.4	95.0	76.2%	28.1%	47.9%

Cubs Prospects

The State of the System:
With the Cubs seemingly prepared to break up their championship core, you may be waiting a while for the farm to produce the next one. There's some interesting talent at the top though.

The Top Ten:

1 ★ ★ ★ *2021 Top 101 Prospect* **#63** ★ ★ ★
Brailyn Marquez   LHP   OFP: 60   ETA: Debuted in 2020
Born: 01/30/99   Age: 22   Bats: L   Throws: L   Height: 6'4"   Weight: 185
Origin: International Free Agent, 2015

The Report: Marquez's September relief cameo pretty well summed up where things stand for him, honestly. His fastball sits in the upper 90s and touches 100, and comes backed by a big, biting slider and a developing changeup. He's battled significant mechanical inconsistencies and wildness during his pro career, and that manifested in his inability to command his fastball at all during his big-league debut. He wasn't ready for the majors, but it was worth a look.

Development Track: Marquez had to be added to the 40-man roster this offseason anyway, so his September appearance only came at the cost of a few days of service time. Although he did not throw it in the majors, he spent a lot of time at the alternate site working on a promising mid-90s sinker.

Variance: High. Marquez still has no real track record of consistently throwing strikes, and until he does there's major bullpen and downside risk.

Mark Barry's Fantasy Take: It's sorta weird that a pitcher who debuted in the majors is still pretty far away, but that's what 2020 will do to a dude like Marquez. All of the upside we loved last year is still there, and this time it's joined by a new sinker. I like the next guy on this list more for fantasy purposes, but Marquez is still a top-100 guy, with one of the most fun ceilings in dynasty.

2 ★ ★ ★ *2021 Top 101 Prospect* **#78** ★ ★ ★
Brennen Davis   CF   OFP: 60   ETA: 2022
Born: 11/02/99   Age: 21   Bats: R   Throws: R   Height: 6'4"   Weight: 175
Origin: Round 2, 2018 Draft (#62 overall)

The Report: "A finger injury limited Davis to just 50 games in 2019, but he showed enough in that abbreviated season to be considered one of the rising stars of the organization. Despite his lack of pro experience, he showed an unexpected polish at the plate, combining contact with natural power. A former prep basketball star, he is built like a shooting guard, but could add good weight to bring more of the power forward. The Cubs will keep him in center as long as they can, and there is a chance he may be able to stick there. However, if a move to a corner spot is necessary, the bat might have enough plus tools in it to carry the load.

Development Track: The lost minor league season might have a silver lining for Davis. Instead of spending a summer in Myrtle Beach, which is extremely hostile to hitters, he faced a steady diet of close-to-major-league ready pitching at the alternate site. Reports out of South Bend tell of a bigger and stronger frame and the ball jumping off the bat. That type of progress in a normal season might have easily put him into the top half of our 101.

Variance: High. Davis still has fewer than 250 professional at bats. It's not a lock he sticks in center, putting a lot of pressure on the hit tool to continue to develop.

Mark Barry's Fantasy Take: You don't have to strain too hard to see a five-category contributor here, and as mentioned above, the lost year of competition might not have been as lost for Davis. He might not stick in center field, but that doesn't really concern me at all. He's a top-30 name for me and if you want to even go a little higher, I wouldn't really argue.

★ ★ ★ *2021 Top 101 Prospect* **#88** ★ ★ ★

3
Ed Howard SS   OFP: 60   ETA: 2024
Born: 08/06/01   Age: 19   Bats: R   Throws: R   Height: 6'2"   Weight: 185
Origin: Round 1, 2020 Draft (#16 overall)

The Report: Last year's draft class skewed heavily to the college side, pushing the consensus top prep infielder in the class—and Chicago native—to the Cubs with the 16th pick. Howard has a projectable 6-foot-2 frame and loose hands that display ahead-of-the-curve contact skills, and there's a belief he will grow into power as the body fills out. There is no denying the glove is ahead of the bat—there's clear present defensive skills at the 6—but that is to be expected and totally fine at present. And even if his final outcome is a glove-first, plus-defender at shortstop, the stick should be more than good enough to justify his presence in the lineup as an everyday starter.

Development Track: While there are some present tools to be excited about, Howard is still very much a freshly-drafted prep bat. His senior spring season was canceled before it started, making it imperative he doesn't lose out on an entire year of much-needed development. Much of the focus for Howard in the next year will be adding strength without losing a step. From a skills standpoint, letting his natural ability play up to a refined pro plate approach won't happen overnight. Patience will be key here, but worth the wait.

Variance: Extreme. Inexperienced prep bats always have inherent risk. Add in the lost senior season and pro summer to COVID-19, and there is further risk of not fully reaching the potential.

Mark Barry's Fantasy Take: Oh hey, there's the cliff.

Admittedly, that's a little unfair to Howard, who I do like. It's just that we haven't seen him play real games since like, the Carter administration. While there are a ton of shortstops out there, Howard's defense will help him stay there long term, where you can expect some top-15 or so production at the six. Or, you know, he could show up as the second-coming of Barry Larkin and we wouldn't have ever known, you know, because of the no games thing.

4 — Miguel Amaya, C — OFP: 60 ETA: Late 2021/Early 2022
Born: 03/09/99 Age: 22 Bats: R Throws: R Height: 6'2" Weight: 230
Origin: International Free Agent, 2015

The Report: In 2019, 20 catchers were worth between 1.5 and 3.0 WARP. Broadly speaking that would be your Role 45-55 catcher tier. You'll find the odd over-performing backup or half-timer—a Will Smith breakout debut mixed in as well—but it's mostly full-time starters. And among that group there's no clear type. Danny Jansen was a defensive specialist with an 82 DRC+, a reverse of his prospect profile. Omar Narváez and Gary Sánchez carried big sticks, but struggled with the defensive load. Robinson Chirinos was pretty average at everything, which of course made him an above-average catcher.

We are writing Amaya as an OFP 60, which means he's likely to fall into that 1.5-3 win group more years than not. What type will he be? Oh, maybe like the good, but declining Yan Gomes seasons. Enough hit tool to get enough of the plus raw pop into play, a solid but not plus-level defender, OBPs that flirt with .300. Amaya does enough things well that you'd expect one of them to stand out enough to make him a solid everyday catcher, but catchers are weird and it's hard to say what that carrying tool will be yet. It's also easy to guess wrong. And there's a chance he stays pretty good at enough stuff to hit that OFP.

Development Track: Amaya spent the summer at the alternate site, mostly because he is quite a good prospect, but also because you always need extra catchers. The quality of arms he would have been facing was broadly Double-A quality or better, so he might be closer to the majors than you'd think for a prospect with no upper minors experience. The reports don't suggest a big move for the profile one way or the other.

Variance: High. Catchers are weird. We might have learned a fair bit about Amaya in Double-A this year instead here we are still writing "Catchers are weird."

Mark Barry's Fantasy Take: *takes a drag of a cigarette, somehow everything is in black and white*

I remember when I liked catching prospects. It was a couple of weeks ago. Amaya is a great real-life catching prospect, but the fantasy variance behind the plate and the ability to find average-ish production on the waiver wire keep him out of my top-200.

5 Adbert Alzolay   RHP   OFP: 55   ETA: Debuted in 2019
Born: 03/01/95   Age: 26   Bats: R   Throws: R   Height: 6'1"   Weight: 208
Origin: International Free Agent, 2012

The Report: Alzolay has bumped up and down these lists for a while, ranking as high as No. 1 in the system and No. 95 on the Top 101 three years ago. The report has never really changed much—plus mid-90s fastball, plus breaking ball (sometimes two), enough change to start—but we've wavered back and forth on whether injuries and command would ultimately limit him to the bullpen.

Development Track: I'm not actually sure 2020 answered those questions in the way we would've liked. Alzolay pitched well in the majors when called upon as an up-and-down swingman type. But he never made it through the order more than twice, and between the short season and his usage we didn't really get any more of an idea if he's a starter or not. The stuff will play in any role, at least.

Variance: Medium. It already looked right in The Show, he just needs to find the right role.

Mark Barry's Fantasy Take: I think Alzolay is probably that guy who gets called on to start games on short notice, but otherwise is a solid multi-inning reliever. He can definitely be useful in that role, but it's not a spot that I would spend a lot of roster capital to fill.

6 Christopher Morel   3B   OFP: 55   ETA: Late 2022/Early 2023
Born: 06/24/99   Age: 22   Bats: R   Throws: R   Height: 6'0"   Weight: 140
Origin: International Free Agent, 2015

The Report: Morel found his way onto the back end of our 2020 Cubs list based on his slick fielding ability and knack for barreling up pitches. He was beginning to catch fire at South Bend, slashing .364/.395/.584 in the second half of 2019, before being sidelined with a fractured knee. The glove is arguably the best in the organization, strong enough for short but potentially elite at third. Offensively, he's still a work in progress, but there's enough potential to project a future major league regular.

Development Track: It was somewhat surprising to see Morel included on the Cubs' alternative site roster due to his relative inexperience. However, the reports from South Bend were glowing about his development. Swing adjustments and physical growth reportedly made for some loud contact and big exit velocity numbers. If the bat is finally catching up, Morel could be on the fast track to Wrigley.

Variance: Medium. Even if the reported offensive strides are a mirage, the glove should be good enough to make him a major league regular.

Mark Barry's Fantasy Take: It would be lovely if Morel's bat caught up to his glove, as his glove is quite good. I wouldn't expect the market for him to be robust right now, so I'd toss him on your watchlist and keep an eye on his first few games. If he's raking, scoop him up before the rest of your league mates know what hit 'em.

7 Kohl Franklin RHP   OFP: 55   ETA: 2024
Born: 09/09/99   Age: 21   Bats: R   Throws: R   Height: 6'4"   Weight: 190
Origin: Round 6, 2018 Draft (#188 overall)

The Report: Franklin had a small breakout in 2019, adding some good weight, some good velocity, and flashing a plus breaking ball. Everything was lined up well for him to have a bigger breakout in 2020 in full-season ball and perhaps move himself into 101 contention and the upper echelon of the system.

Development Track: Franklin wasn't included in the alternate site or instructional league roster. So we have little actionable info. He's hardly the only prospect in this boat, but it's particularly annoying given the shallowness of the Cubs' system.

Variance: High. 2020 is a lost developmental year and the risks here were already on the high side.

Mark Barry's Fantasy Take: Last season, Ben mentioned that we were a year away from really knowing Franklin's fantasy value. So, about that ... it's not ideal, but it also means we're all in the same boat as far as Franklin's development is concerned.

8 Ryan Jensen RHP   OFP: 55   ETA: 2022 as a reliever, 2023 as a starter
Born: 11/23/97   Age: 23   Bats: R   Throws: R   Height: 6'0"   Weight: 180
Origin: Round 1, 2019 Draft (#27 overall)

The Report: Jensen had a dominant junior season at Fresno State on the back of his explosive fastball/slider combo, but it was his only college season as a full-time starter and the only one where he was able to tame his high-effort mechanics from a command and control standpoint. There was significant reliever risk given the size and delivery—and the needed changeup development—but the Cubs appeared to see him as a starter, and the stuff should have dominated A-ball in 2020, but well, you know.

Development Track: Jensen wasn't included in the alternate site or instructional league roster. So we have little actionable info. He's hardly the only prospect in this boat, but it's particularly annoying given the shallowness of the Cubs system.

Variance: High. There was significant profile risk coming out of college, and you would have liked to have Jensen just work on his changeup in real games for a year. He could move quickly as a reliever but everything is an open-ended question until April 2021.

Mark Barry's Fantasy Take: What's the expression about square pegs in round holes? That you don't need to worry about them in a fantasy sense unless they turn into round pegs?

9 Yohendrick Pinango   OF   OFP: 55   ETA: 2025
Born: 05/07/02   Age: 19   Bats: L   Throws: L   Height: 5'11"   Weight: 170
Origin: International Free Agent, 2018

The Report: Pinango wasn't the biggest name or biggest bonus out of the Cubs 2018 IFA class, but he may be the most advanced hitter at present.

Development Track: Pinango was one of the youngest Cubs in Mesa for instructs, and he acquitted himself well, showing advanced bat-to-ball skills and hard contact against higher-level arms, although the swing isn't currently geared for power. Pinango has played mostly corner outfield so far, although the team believes with more time in a pro strength and conditioning program he could work himself into a passable center fielder.

Variance: Extreme. He hasn't played outside of a complex and might be a corner outfielder who hasn't started lifting the ball yet. The hitting ability suggests he isn't a mere lottery ticket, but everything in the profile is a long way from actualizing.

Mark Barry's Fantasy Take: While his name might suggest a star Quidditch player for the Chudley Cannons, I'm intrigued by Pinango and his contact ability. He's one for the watchlist right now, but he's a teenage-J2 guy putting up gaudy stolen base numbers, so he'll be super trendy if he hits early. You'll need to move fast.

10 Burl Carraway   LHP   OFP: 55   ETA: 2021
Born: 05/27/99   Age: 22   Bats: L   Throws: L   Height: 6'0"   Weight: 173
Origin: Round 2, 2020 Draft (#51 overall)

The Report: Prior to the 2020 draft, one Texas-area scout said Carraway would be the first player in the class to make it to the big leagues. Even though a different power lefty playing on the South Side of Chicago officially holds that title, Carraway is still viewed by many as a quick-moving reliever who should crack the Cubs' bullpen sooner rather than later. Not the biggest guy you see with a power fastball, he manages to get good plane on the mid-to-high 90s pitch thanks to an over-the-top slot. Paired with a big bending curveball, the two-pitch mix with plus grades should function well in high leverage situations provided the command improves.

Development Track: It certainly is swing-and-miss stuff, with the clear areas of improvement being command of the curveball and control of the fastball. He can get away with attacking hitters earlier in the count to get ahead, then finishing off the plate to get hitters to chase. Where he gets into trouble is getting behind in the count and having to make higher quality pitches. If he shows he can limit the free passes he will be knocking on the door of the Wrigley Field home clubhouse in no time.

Variance: High. The fastball/curve combo is so good you don't want to sacrifice too much of the dynamic nature of the pitches to shift a gear down for a better idea where it's going.

Mark Barry's Fantasy Take: The question with Carraway will be whether he can strike out enough guys to stay useful without saves, or multiple-inning outings. It's possible, but it's an awfully small needle to thread. I'll pass.

The Prospects You Meet Outside The Top Ten:

High upside, but a ways away

Rafael Morel SS Born: 11/22/01 Age: 19 Bats: R Throws: R Height: 5'11" Weight: 165 Origin: International Free Agent, 2018
The Cubs signed the younger Morel brother in the summer of 2018, out of the Dominican Republic for $850,000. Thinly built, Rafael mirrors older brother Chris' prowess on the left side of the diamond and with his ability to make contact. He currently lacks for pop offensively but his feel for hitting and ability to stick at short will buy him time for it to develop.

Interesting draft follows

Jordan Nwogu Born: 03/10/99 Age: 22 Bats: R Throws: R Height: 6'3" Weight: 235 Origin: Round 3, 2020 Draft (#88 overall)
Featuring the type of frame and strength you wish you could clone for every outfielder, Nwogu has first-round tools. He wasn't selected until the third round because his swing mechanics are a work-in-progress (to put it lightly) that were in a constant state of flux during his time at the University of Michigan. Once in the hitting lab with his new coaches, he'll need to find a comfortable setup that maximizes his ability to hit the ball hard, getting him shorter to the ball with better hand placement and no wasted movement.

Luke Little Born: 08/30/00 Age: 20 Bats: L Throws: L Height: 6'8" Weight: 225 Origin: Round 4, 2020 Draft (#117 overall)

Little was a little-known junior college pitcher committed to South Carolina when he hit 105 in May. Granted, it was an indoor bullpen session with a Pocket Radar, so not exactly game conditions, and he walked nearly a batter an inning during his junior college career, mostly out of the 'pen. But still, 105 is 105, and when it's coming from a 6-foot-8 left…

Top Talents 25 and Under (as of 4/1/2021):

1. Brailyn Marquez, LHP
2. Brennen Davis, OF
3. Nico Hoerner, 2B/SS
4. Ed Howard, SS
5. Miguel Amaya, C
6. Christopher Morel, 3B
7. Kohl Franklin, RHP
8. Ryan Jense, RHP
9. Yohendrick Pinango, OF
10. Burl Carraway, LHP

Just one shout here, but it's a pretty good one. Nico Hoerner was the top prospect in this system and No. 41 in baseball last year. He almost retained prospect eligibility this year, so we did some initial evaluation work on him. We're moderately concerned that his hit tool didn't show up much at all in 2020. We never expected big power out of the profile, but we did expect more than four extra-base hits in 126 plate appearances. It was a weird season where he didn't truly get regular playing time and bounced around the diamond, but we did think he was more ready than he looked and his stock is down a bit. We're still cautiously optimistic overall, though.

Part 3: Featured Articles

Cubs All-Time Top 10 Players

by Matthew Trueblood

POSITION PLAYERS

GABBY HARTNETT, C (1922–1940)
The leader and lineup linchpin of the longest-running successful Cubs teams in history, Hartnett won one MVP award and could have won a couple more. He had a rocket arm behind the plate; at bat he was a patience-and-power machine. Few catchers, even with modern sports medicine and equipment, have enjoyed as long a career as Hartnett did. In the twilight of his career, he even served as a player-manager and won a pennant.

FRANK CHANCE, 1B/C (1898–1912)
Famously tough, Chance would have become more of a legend if he'd striven to be respected for anything besides resilience, because ultimately he was as vulnerable to the cumulative weight of his injuries. He was hit by pitches 137 times in a career that spanned only 5,135 plate appearances. His career was so attenuated largely because some of those plunkings were in inconvenient places, such as his head). When he kept his body out of the path of the ball long enough to stay out of the path of the ball, Chance slickly fielded first base, walked often, and hit .296 with good power for the period. For much of his career, he was a player-manager, and "peerless" leadership became as much a part of his legacy as his skills.

MARK GRACE, 1B (1988–2000)
No one had more hits (or more doubles) in the 1990s. That's the kind of statistic that can mislead if you let it, but it says something true about Grace. He was an exceptional contact hitter with a discerning eye. He rarely muscled up to yank a ball over the fence, but had sensational bat control and could shoot either gap. His swing was simultaneously elegant and awkward, with his legs doing almost

no work and his torso leaning as much or as little as he needed in order to reach the ball with the sweet spot on his lumber. Lead-legged on the bases, he was light-footed and soft-handed around first base, and the sum of his parts was a stellar, well-rounded, old-school first baseman. Somehow the Cubs never saw him as the leadoff or no. 2 hitter he was born to be.

RYNE SANDBERG, 2B (1982–1994, 1996–1997)

With great speed and above-average power, Sandberg was the kind of balanced star teams and fans most loved during the 1980s. He didn't walk much, but he made plenty of contact to press the issue with his legs, and in his later prime, he developed pop not seen from a second baseman in the previous half-century. A famous errorless streak led some to overrate his glove, but it was true that he showed light feet and soft hands at the keystone. He declined quickly in his mid-30s, but not before blazing a trail for a new breed at his position. The trade that brought him from the Phillies (with Larry Bowa, for shortstop Ivan de Jesus) remains one of the most lopsided in the history of the game.

STAN HACK, 3B (1932–1947)

"Smilin' Stan" didn't hit for power but that was his only true weakness. A lefty-swinging third baseman, he hit .301 and got on base at a .394 clip over a long career. He hardly ever struck out and walked at a sterling rate. As one of the National League's greatest leadoff hitters he scored 100 or more runs in a season seven times. Thanks in part to being too old to be called away to serve in World War II, he declined gracefully, and was a key cog even on the team's 1945 pennant winner.

RON SANTO, 3B (1960–1973)

No more well-rounded player ever put on the Cubs' uniform. At his peak, Santo was a deserving Gold Glove winner at third base with a strong arm and quick reflexes. At the plate, he had excellent plate discipline, leading the National League in walks four times in five seasons from 1964-68. When he did elect to swing, it was a lashing, pull-conscious uppercut, producing 25-30 home runs per year throughout his peak, and as many doubles. He did it all despite having Type 1 diabetes, a condition much more limiting in the 1960s than it is today, something he didn't reveal until late in his career.

JOE TINKER, SS (1902–1912, 1916)

Probably the only member of the famous double-play combination whose defensive chops were everything FPA's verse implied them up to be, Tinker was also a fine hitter for a shortstop of his era. Aggressive at the plate, he put the ball in play, but also generated solid gap power relative to the Deadball Era.

ERNIE BANKS, SS/1B (1953–1971)

The transformative power of excellence: The first Black player in franchise history retired with the nickname "Mr. Cub." Banks was a shortstop ahead of his time, posing an unprecedented power threat at what had traditionally been a position of good-field/no-hit players. He assumed an imperious posture at the plate, leaning out over the dish with his back elbow up, pulling his hands down to wind his bat up, then unleashing it on the ball with tremendous force. Knee trouble turned him from a brilliant defensive shortstop in his late 20s to a first baseman at age 30, and the final decade of his career was thoroughly unspectacular, but Banks had left his mark.

BILLY WILLIAMS, OF (1959–1974)

Williams was the most underrated slugger of his generation. Overshadowed in turns by both Santo and Banks and playing in an era dominated by pitchers, Williams was often a better hitter than either. The only great left-handed power hitter in team history, he was even more of a standout than his raw numbers suggest. He drew 1,045 walks and struck out just 1,046 times for his career, and from his first full season through his retirement, only Hank Aaron had more extra-base hits. Williams was also an iron man, not missing a game for almost a decade.

SAMMY SOSA, OF (1992–2004)

Few players have had their greatness more unfairly dismissed because of PED allegations than has Sosa. An extraordinarily toolsy young player, he was a big-league regular by the time he was 21. By 24, he was a brilliant defensive right fielder who blended power and speed at the plate. When he turned the corner five years later, good health and expansion played at least as big a role as any injectables. Sosa was eminently watchable. His personality was infused into even routine baseball actions communicating to fans how much he appreciated baseball. Now that he's retired, baseball—that is, Baseball—refused to reciprocate.

PITCHERS

THREE FINGER BROWN, RHP (1904–1912, 1916)

Brown had an ERA under 2.00 every season from 1906 through 1910, exemplary even by the standards of the Deadball Era. He averaged 292 innings pitched per year and had an aggregate ERA of 1.42 over the span. His hand, badly mangled in two distinct childhood accidents, allowed him to throw what was arguably the best curveball of his time. It was a big, overhand hook and hitters had never seen anything like it. Though he didn't debut until 26, Brown pitched almost 3,200 innings and racked up 239 wins, 188 of them for the Cubs.

HIPPO VAUGHN, LHP (1913–1921)

He probably preferred his other nickname, Big Jim, but Vaughn battled weight trouble throughout his career. He had failed to follow up on a dominant rookie season with the 1910 Highlanders and the Cubs had to rescue him from the minors in 1913. He took off, averaging 293 innings for half a decade and change. He won 22 games, the ERA and strikeout titles, and led the National League in innings pitched in 1918, the same year he pitched three times for the Cubs in the World Series. He was a five-time 20-game winner overall, though his 1915 season is instructive in that he piled up the victories despite an ERA above league average. Within three years, though, he'd let his conditioning lapse again, and he crashed out of baseball at the age of 33. Claim to immortality: On May 2, 1917 tied up with the Reds' Fred Toney in a double no-hitter, both pitchers putting up blanks through nine. Vaughn gave up a couple of hits and a run in the 10th and Toney completed his no-hit shutout in the bottom of the inning.

PETE ALEXANDER, RHP (1918–1926)

Few players of his time threw as hard as Alexander. None did so from the abbreviated, truly sidearm angle Alexander used. He called his signature offering a curveball, but it was a sharpish one, and given his arm angle, it behaved much like a slider. Using that angle, power, and his unique break, he won six strikeout titles, all in his first 10 seasons. He was never the same thereafter—still a good pitcher, but nowhere near as dominant, and without the ability to miss bats. The Cubs were just a bridge team in his career—they acquired him when parsimonious Phillies ownership dumped him when they realized he'd be lost to World War I military service—though they still got a few of his best years before conflicts with manager Joe McCarthy ended his tenure.

CHARLIE ROOT, RHP (1926–1941)

Known as an especially nasty sidearmer and a very uncomfortable at-bat, Root took pride in changing speeds, the shape of each of his pitches, and his arm angle, believing that was the way to keep hitters on the defensive. Over his first eight seasons with the Cubs, he averaged 252 innings a year and was a solid front-of-the-rotation starter if never a true ace. He pitched in all four of Chicago's World Series appearances from 1929-1938 (going 0-3 with a 6.75 ERA in six games), but his most famous moment in them was as the pitcher who gave up Babe Ruth's called shot—not that he would admit that Ruth had truly called it.

CLAUDE PASSEAU, RHP (1939–1947)

A late bloomer who first found (some) success with the Phillies, Passeau took full advantage of the war years and made four All-Star teams for the Cubs, for whom he pitched from 1940 through the end of his career. On a hunting trip during his teens, a misfired shotgun badly injured his left (non-throwing) hand, and because of that, Passeau was allowed to keep his glove on when rubbing up the ball on the mound. That, plus the devastating action on his sinker, led many to accuse him of throwing a spitball, though Passeau never admitted to doing so. He did thoroughly excel at keeping the ball in the ballpark, be it wet or dry. As with many other Cubs' greats, Passeau had previously been property of the Phillies, but this trade wasn't as unbalanced as some others; the Cubs gave up a good pitcher, Kirby Higbe.

BOB RUSH, RHP (1948-1957)

Many older, established ballplayers spent World War II serving their country by playing ball to boost the morale of fighting men. Rush, who was just shy of 16 when Pearl Harbor was bombed, wasn't so lucky. He spent much of 1944 and the first half of 1945 as a teenaged machine gunner pushing through Germany. After that, he deserved a career of good breaks and good ballclubs. Instead, he signed with the Cubs. Notwithstanding the arrival and ascendance of Banks, the decade Rush spent in Chicago happened to be the most moribund in team history. He lost 140 games despite being an above-average pitcher. Huge for his time and blessed with a blazing fastball, Rush was perfectly solid. He just never had sufficient offensive or defensive support to make it matter.

FERGUSON JENKINS, RHP (1966–1973, 1982–1983)

Though he lacked a single dominant offering, Jenkins was a dominant pitcher. He had excellent control and threw the kitchen sink at opponents: sinker, four-seamer, slider, curve, forkball. Every year from 1967 through 1972 he won at least 20 games, completed at least 20 games, and pitched at least 289 innings. Though he was much less brilliant in his 30s, he remained durable and finished his career with 4,500 innings, in total. Another lopsided trade with the Phillies brought him to Chicago; the one that sent him to the Rangers for his final 20-win season wasn't nearly so unbalanced, returning two-time Cubs batting-title winner Bill Madlock.

RICK REUSCHEL, RHP (1972–1981, 1983–1984)

He was the starter who wouldn't go away. Reuschel, like Jenkins, was a stellar workhorse in his 20s, averaging 245 innings a year from 1973-1980. Despite injuries putting his career on life support two or three times, he held on for a decade as an overqualified journeyman. As great pitchers must, he reinvented himself over the years, going to a slider/cutter late in his career to make up for his lost ability to miss bats with his fastball and curve. An excellent athlete despite a zaftig physique, had he pitched for better teams he would have been a serious Hall of Fame candidate.

GREG MADDUX, RHP (1986–1992, 2004–2006)
Maddux was arguably the greatest pitcher of all time. Alas, most of his best seasons came in Atlanta. He took his lumps on bad Cubs teams at 20 and 21, but by the late 1980s, he was one of the game's premier young starters. His surgical command came to him only at the tail end of his first Cubs stint and his ability to miss bats had deserted him by his second, but his perfect, seemingly effortless mechanics were there almost all along, allowing him to be the great workhorse of his era. He won the first of his four straight Cy Young Awards as a Cub in 1992 and his 300th game with the team in 2004.

CARLOS ZAMBRANO, RHP (2001–2011)
"Big Z' was big in every sense. Had he come along even a half-decade later, his early workload would have been managed much more carefully; his eclectic, often chaotic pitch mix would have been streamlined; and someone would have demanded that he throw more strikes. As it was, he staged a once-weekly Evel Knievel show in place of a typical baseball game. He threw hard, induced tons of grounders, and could wipe people out with his splitter or slider at times. He also walked at least 100 batters in a season (twice), was unafraid to hit batters, and let his emotions control him, often leading to a dramatic unraveling. A power-hitter by the standards of pitchers, he slugged .388 lifetime, fourth among postwar pitchers with at least 100 plate appearances.

A Taxonomy of 2020 Abnormalities

by Rob Mains

I'm going to start this with a trivia question. Trust me, it's relevant. Don't bother skipping to the end of the article to find the answer, it's not there.

Only five players have appeared in 140 or more games for 16 straight seasons. Who are they?

It's a trivia question starting off an essay, so you know how this works: Whatever you guessed, you're wrong. It's okay. As someone who purchased this book, chances are good that you're an educated baseball fan. But the circumstances behind 2020 force us to abandon, or at least seriously question, some of our favorite patterns and crutches for evaluating the game we love.

We just completed what was undoubtedly the strangest season in MLB history. No fans, geographically limited schedule, universal DH, seven-inning twin bills, runners on second in extra innings, a 16-team postseason, a club playing at a Triple-A stadium. Some of these changes will likely persist (sorry), but we've never had so many tweaks dumped on us all at once, at least not since they figured out how many balls were in a walk.

And the biggest, of course, was the 60-game season. The 19th century was dotted with teams that went bankrupt before the season ended, but the lone season with only 60 scheduled games was 1877. That year there were only six teams, the league rostered a total of 77 players (just 16 more than the 2020 Marlins), and batters called for pitches to be thrown high or low by the pitcher, who was 50 feet away. We can say the 2020 season was easily the shortest ever for recognizable baseball.

As such, it'll stand out. Few abbreviated seasons do. Just about everybody reading this knows the 1994 season ended after Seattle's Randy Johnson struck out Oakland's Ernie Young for the last out of the Mariners-A's game on August 11. The ensuing player strike wiped out the rest of the season and the postseason. Teams played only 112-117 games that year.

And many of you know that a strike in the middle of the 1981 season split the season in two, resulting in the only Division Series until 1995. Teams played only 103-111 games that year, the shortest regular season since 1885.

Those two seasons are memorable. So when we see that nobody drove in 100 runs in 1981, or that Greg Maddux was the only pitcher with 180 or more innings pitched in 1994, we think, "Of course. Strike year."

But we don't remember other short years. You might not recall that the 1994 strike spilled into the next year, chopping 18 games off the 1995 schedule. You might've read that the 1918 season, played during the last pandemic, ended after Labor Day due to the government's World War I "work or fight" order. A strike erased the first week and a half of the 1972 season, but that year's best known as the last time pitchers batted in the American League.

The point is, while we don't remember small changes to the schedule, we remember the big ones. The 1981 mid-season strike. The 1994 season- and Series-ending strike. And, of course, the pandemic-shortened 2020 season. We won't need a reminder why Marcell Ozuna's 18 homers were the fewest to lead the National League in a century. (Literally; Cy Williams led with 15 in 1920.)

Now, about that trivia question. The five players are Hank Aaron, Brooks Robinson, Pete Rose, Ichiro Suzuki, and Johnny Damon. The one nobody gets, of course, is Damon, and a lot of people miss Ichiro, whose last season of 140-plus games came garbed in the red-orange and ocean blue of Miami when he was 42. That's half of what makes it a good question. The other half is the two guys whom many think made the list but didn't. Lou Gehrig? His streak started in the Yankees' 42nd game of the 1925 season and lasted only 13 seasons after that. And everybody assumes Cal Ripken Jr. did it, having played 2,632 straight games over 17 seasons. But one of those 17 seasons was 1994, when the Orioles played only 112 games.

My point? *I just told you* everybody remembers the 1994 strike year, but everybody forgets it fell in the middle of Ripken's streak, separating the first twelve years from the last four. Just because we recall something doesn't mean it's always at the front of our minds.

Nobody is going to forget 2020, and baseball is obviously not the main reason. But there will come a time in the future when you're looking at a player's or a team's record, and there will be baffling numbers there for 2020, and you'll think, "I wonder what happened." (Not to mention the missing line for minor league players.) Just like you forgot that the 1994 strike limited Ripken to 112 games.

Try not to forget it, though. The 2020 season resulted in weird statistical results for several reasons.

There were only 60 games.
I know, duh. But that had impacts beyond counting stats like Ozuna's home run total or Yu Darvish and Shane Bieber leading the majors with eight wins. (I know, pitcher wins, but still.)

The 162-game season is the longest among major North American sports, and that duration gives us a gift. Over the course of a long season, small variations tend to even out. A player who has a ten-game hot streak will probably have a ten-game cold streak. A team that starts the year losing a bunch of close games will probably win a bunch of them. We get regression to the mean. Statistics stabilize.

Consider flipping a coin. Over the long run, we expect it to come up heads about half the time. But the fewer flips, the more variation there'll be. If you flip a coin six times, probability theory tells us you'll get at least two-third heads about 34 percent of the time. Flip it 30 times, your chance of two-thirds heads drops to five percent.

Or, relevant to this case, if you flip a coin 60 times, your chance of getting at least 36 heads—that's 60 percent—is 7.75 percent. Expand the coin-flipping to 162 times, and the chance of getting 60 percent heads drops to 0.73 percent.

In other words, the odds of an outcome that's 20 percent better (or worse) than expected is *more than ten times higher* when you flip your coin 60 times than when you do it 162 times. Call it small sample size, call lack of mean reversion, or call it luck not evening out, 162 is a lot more predictive than 60. You get much more variation over 60 games than over 162. Bieber's 1.63 ERA and 0.87 FIP aren't something we'd see over a full season, and neither is Javier Baéz's .203/.238/.360.

Some players' lines in 2020 look normal. Brian Anderson had an .811 OPS in 2019 and an .810 OPS in 2020. (He probably would have gotten that last point if he'd been given enough time.) But there are many like Bieber and Baéz, some of them from young players still establishing their talent levels. The answer to the question, "What went right or wrong for that guy in 2020?" is most likely "Nothing, it was just a 2020 thing."

Preseason training was abbreviated for hitters.

Every year, spring training drags. Players get tired of it, fans get tired of it, and you sure can tell sportswriters get tired of it. Yes, something to get everyone into shape is necessary, but does it really have to drag on for over a month? Can't we shorten it?

The 2020 season answered in the negative, at least for hitters. Warren Spahn is credited with saying that hitting is timing and pitching is upsetting timing. It appears nobody had his timing down after the abbreviated July summer camp. Through August 9—18 games into the season—MLB batters were hitting .230/.311/.395 with a .275 BABIP. That BABIP, had it held, would have been the lowest since 1968, the Year of the Pitcher. In recent years it's hovered around .300.

It didn't hold. Play returned to more normal levels the rest of the year: .249/.325/.425 with a .297 BABIP starting August 10. But batters whose play concentrated in those first two weeks wound up with ugly lines. Andrew

Benintendi went on the injured list with a season-ending rib cage strain on August 11. His final line: .103/.314/.128 in 14 games. Franchy Cordero went on the IL with a hamate bone fracture on August 9 and a .154/.185/.231 line. Even though he came back strong in a late September return, it was too late to repair his full-season numbers.

Preseason training was abbreviated for pitchers.

Every year, spring training drags. Players get tired of it, fans get tired of it … wait, I already said that. But the abbreviated preseason was tough on pitchers, too. As noted, they had the upper hand coming out of the gate. But then they lost that hand. And then their arms, too.

The 2020 season was spread over 67 days. During those 67 days, 237 pitchers hit the Injured List, compared to 135 in the first 67 days of 2019. A lot of those IL stints, though, were COVID-19-related. Still, over the first 67 days of the 2019 season, there were 72 pitchers on the IL with arm injuries. That figure jumped to 110 in 2020, a 53 percent increase.

There are a number of factors contributing to pitcher arm injuries, ranging from usage to velocity, but it appears that attenuated preseason training played a role. A lot of pitchers had super-short seasons due to arm woes. Corey Kluber, Roberto Osuna, and Shohei Ohtani combined for seven innings, none after August 8. All suffered arm injuries. We'll never know whether they'd have fared better with a longer preseason, but we can guess how they probably feel.

Everybody played.

Rosters were set to expand from 25 to 26 in 2020, so even if we'd had a normal season, we'd have likely seen 2019's record of 1,410 players on MLB rosters broken. But due to the pandemic, rosters started the year at 30 and were cut to only 28. Add multiple COVID-19 absences and the revolving door caused by poor starts by hitters and a rash of pitcher arm injuries, and 1,289 players appeared in MLB games in 2020. The comparable figure over the first 67 days of the 2019 season was 1,109. That 16 percent increase works out to an average of six more players per team in 2020 compared to a similar slice of 2019. A future look back at 2020 rosters will include a lot of unfamiliar names.

Plus became a minus.

In advanced metrics, we adjust batter and pitcher performance for park and league/era variations. A plus sign appended to the end of a measure means that it's adjusted for park and league. It's scaled to an average of 100, with higher figures above average and lower figures below average. (Similarly, a metric with a minus is also park- and league-adjusted and scaled to 100, with lower values better.) Here at BP, our advanced measure of offensive performance is DRC+. Baseball-Reference has OPS+ and FanGraphs has wRC+.

Using park and league adjustments, we can compare Dante Bichette's 1995 Steroid Era season at pre-humidor Coors Field (.340/.364/.620, 40 homers, 128 RBI, MVP runner-up) with Jim Wynn's 1968 Year of the Pitcher season at the cavernous Astrodome (.269/.376/.474, 26 homers, 67 RBI, no MVP votes). It's not close. DRC+, OPS+, and wRC+ all give the nod to Wynn, handily. This is a useful tool. As my Baseball Prospectus colleague Patrick Dubuque tweeted last fall, "Please note that when I ask how you are, I am already adjusting for era."

The 2020 season messes up plus (and minus) stats for two reasons. First, the park adjustment was based on only 30 home games instead of the usual 81. Everything noted above regarding the short season applies, literally doubly, to park effect calculations. DRC+ uses a single-season park factor. OPS+ uses a three-year average and wRC+ five years. The figure for 2020 is suspect.

Second, OPS+ and wRC+ adjust for league: American and National. (DRC+ adjusts for opponent, regardless of league.) While there were two leagues in 2020, they were an artificial construct. To reduce travel, teams played opponents geographically, not based on league. There weren't two leagues, American and National. There were three, Western, Central, and Eastern.

That makes a difference because teams in the same league played in different run-scoring environments. AL teams scored 4.58 runs per game, NL teams 4.71. That's a small difference. But teams in the East scored 0.21 more runs per game (4.95) than teams in the West (4.74), and they both scored a lot more than Central teams (4.25). Adjusting for league misses that difference, so this book will be safe in that regard, but other sources may be distorted somewhat.

Not every game was a "game."
In 2020, the rising tide of strikeouts was finally stemmed. Strikeouts per team per game fell from 8.8 in 2019 to 8.7 in 2020. That marked the first decline after 14 straight annual increases.

In 2020, the rising tide of strikeouts rose higher. Batters struck out in 23.4 percent of plate appearances compared to 23.0 percent in 2019. That marked the 15th straight annual increase.

Both are true statements.

Because of two rule changes—seven-inning doubleheaders and runners on second in extra innings—games in 2020 were unprecedented in their brevity. There were 37.0 plate appearances per game in 2020. The only years with fewer were 1904 and 1906-1909. The average game in 2020 entailed 8.61 innings pitched, the fewest since 1899.

So when you see any per-game stats for 2020, you need to increase them by 3 or 4 percent to get them on equal footing with recent years.

Or, better, just ignore them. Last year happened. There were major league games contested between major league teams. But when you're looking at those physical or electronic baseball cards, when you're weaving narratives over why this young player's inevitable rise to stardom fell apart or why that old veteran rekindled his magic, don't linger on the 2020 line. It was just too weird.

Thanks to Lucas Apostoleris for research assistance.

—*Rob Mains is an author of Baseball Prospectus.*

Tranches of WAR

by Russell A. Carleton

We ask "replacement level" to be a lot of things. Sometimes contradictory things. Sometimes I wonder if we know what it even means anymore. The original idea was that it represented the level of production that a team could expect to get from "freely available talent", including bench players, minor leaguers, and waiver wire pickups. It created a common benchmark to compare everyone to, and for that reason, it represented an advancement well beyond what was available at the time. In fact, it created a language and a framework for evaluating players that was not just better but *entirely* different than what came before it.

But then we started mumbling in that language. The idea behind "wins above replacement" was one part sci-fi episode and one part mathematical exercise. Imagine that a player had disappeared before the season and suddenly, in an alternate timeline, his team would have had to replace him. The distance between him and that replacement line was his value. We need to talk about that alternate timeline.

Without getting too into 2:00 am "deep conversations" with extensive navel-gazing, it's worth thinking about why one player might not be playing, while another might.

- A player might not be playing because he has a short-term injury or his manager believes that he needs a day off.
- A player might not be playing because he has a longer-term injury that requires him to be on the injured list.

There's a difference here between these two situations. In particular, the first one generally *doesn't* involve a compensatory roster move, while the second one does. It's possible, though not guaranteed, that the person who will be replacing the injured/resting player would be the same in either case. That matters. Teams generally carry a spare part for all eight position players on the diamond, although in the era of a four-player bench, those spare parts usually are the backup plan for more than one spot.

A couple of years ago, I posed a hypothetical question. Suppose that a team had two players in its system fighting for a fourth outfielder spot. One of them was a league average hitter, but would be worth 20 runs below average if allowed to play center field for a full season. One of them was a perfectly average fielder, but would be 15 runs below average as a hitter, if allowed to play an entire season. Which of the two should the team roster? It's tempting to say the second one, as overall, he is the better player. That misses the point. A league average hitter on the bench isn't just a potential replacement for an injured outfielder. He might also pinch hit for the light-hitting shortstop in a key spot. You keep the average hitter on the roster, even though he isn't a hand-in-glove fit for one specific place on the field, because being a bench player is a different job description than being a long-term fill-in for someone. If you find yourself in need of a longer-term fill-in, you can bring the other guy up from AAA.

When we're determining the value of an everyday player though, if he had disappeared before the season and a team would have had to replace his production, they likely would have done it with a player who was a long-term fill-in type because they would have had to replace a guy who played everyday. Maybe that's the same guy that they would have rostered on their bench anyway, but we don't know. It gets to the query of what we hope to accomplish with WAR. Are we looking for an accurate modeling of reality or are we looking for a common baseline to compare everyone to? Both have their uses, but they are somewhat different questions.

Let's talk about another dichotomy.

- A player might not be playing because he isn't very good and is a bench-level player.
- A player might not be playing because there is another player on the team who has a situational advantage that makes him the better choice today. The classic case of this is a handedness platoon. On another day, he might be a better choice.

When we think about player usage, I think we're still stuck in the model that there are starters and there are scrubs. We have plenty of words for bench players or reserves or backups or utility guys. We do still have the word "platoon" in our collective vocabulary, but in the age of short benches, it's hard to construct one. It's always been hard to construct them. You have to find two players who hit with different hands, have skill sets that complement each other, and probably play the same position. In the era of the short bench, one of them had probably better double as a utility player in some way. Baseball has a two-tiered language geared toward the idea of regulars and reserves. The fact that it was so easy for me to find plenty of synonyms for "a player whose primary function is to come into a game to replace a regular player if he is injured or resting" should tell you something.

I'm always one to look for "unspoken words" in baseball. What is it called when someone is both half of a platoon and the utility infielder? That guy exists sometimes, but he reveals himself in that role—usually by accident. We don't have a word for that, and whenever I find myself saying "we don't have a word for that", I look for new opportunities. What do you call it, further, when the job of being the utility infielder is decentralized across the whole infield with occasional contributions from the left fielder? It's not even a "super-utility" player. What happens when you build your entire roster around the idea that everyone will be expected to be a triple major?

⚾ ⚾ ⚾

I think someone else beat me to this one, and on a grand scale. Platoons work because we know that hitters of the opposite hand to the pitcher get better results than hitters of the same hand, usually to the tune of about 20 points of OBP. If you want to express that in runs, it usually comes out to somewhere around 10 to 12 runs of linear weights value prorated across 650 PA. But hang on a second, now let's say that we have two players who might start today, both of roughly equal merit with the bat. One has a handedness advantage, but is the worse fielder of the two. In that case, as long as his "over the course of a season" projection as a fielder at whatever position you want to slot him into is less than a 10-run drop from the guy he might replace, then he's a better option today.

We're not used to thinking of utility players as bat-first options, who would play below-average defense at three different infield positions. That guy might hook on as a 2B/3B/LF type (Howie Kendrick, come on down!) but teams usually think to themselves that they need as their utility infielder someone who "can handle" shortstop, the toughest of the infield spots to play. If someone can do that *and* hit well, he's probably already starting somewhere, so he's not available as a utility infielder. It's easier for those glove guys to find a job. In a world where the replacement for a shortstop *has to be* the designated utility infielder, that makes sense.

But as we talked about last week, we're living in a different world. The rate at which a replacement for a regular starter turns out to be *another starter* shifting over to cover has gone way up over the last five years. There was always some of it in the game, but this has been a supernova of switcheroos. Now if your second baseman is capable of playing a decent shortstop, that 2B/3B/LF guy can swap in. He's not actually playing shortstop, and maybe the defense suffers from the switch, but if he's got enough of a bat, he might outhit those extra fielding miscues. And in doing so, he is effectively your backup shortstop.

Somewhere along the lines, teams got hip to the idea of multi-positional play from their regulars. I've written before about how you can't just put a player, however athletic, into a new position and expect much at first. The data tell us that. Eventually, players can learn to be multi-positionalists, but it takes time, roughly on the order of two months, before they're OK. But there's a hidden message in there. If you give a player some reps at a new spot, he's a reasonably gifted athlete and somewhat smart and willing to learn, he could probably pick it up enough to get to "good enough," and it doesn't take forever. You just have to be purposeful about it. Maybe you get to the point where you can start to say "he's still below average but we could move him there and get another bat into the lineup, and it's a net win."

Teams have started to build those extra lessons into their player development program. It used to be seen as a mark of weakness to be relegated to "utility player" because that meant that you were a bench player (all those synonyms above come with a side of stigma). Now, it's a way of building a team. If you get a few reps in the minors (where it doesn't count) at a spot, you'll have at least played the spot at game speed before. There are limits to how far you can push that. A slow-footed "he's out in left field because we don't have the DH" guy is never going to play short, but maybe your third baseman can try second base and not look like a total moose out there.

⚾ ⚾ ⚾

Back to WAR. I'd argue that the world of starters and scrubs is slowly disintegrating, for good cause. In the event that a regular starter really does go down with an injury–ostensibly, the alternate universe scenario that WAR is attempting to model–it makes the team a little more resilient to replacing him. And the good news is that you're more likely to be able to replace him with the best of the bench bunch, rather than the third-best guy, because the best guy doesn't have to be an exact positional match for the guy who got hurt. And that's what the manager would want to do. He'd want to replace that long-term production, not with an amalgam of everyone else who played that position, but with the best guy available from his reserves.

Now this is still WAR. We still want to retain the principle that we should be measuring a player, and not his teammates. We need some sort of common baseline, and despite what I just said, we'll still need some sort of amalgam. To construct that, I give to you the idea of the tranche. The word, if you've not heard it before, refers to a piece of a whole that is somehow segmented off. It's often used in finance to talk about layers of a financial instrument.

Here, I want you to consider that there are 30 starters at each of the seven non-battery positions (catchers should have their own WAR, since only a catcher can replace a catcher). We can identify them by playing time, and we can futz around with the definition a little bit if we need to. Next, among those who aren't in that starting pool, we identify the top tranche of the 30 best bench players, which I would again identify by playing time, and then the second and third and fourth and so on. If a player were to disappear, his manager would probably want to take a guy from that top tranche of the bench to replace him. In a world where even the starters can slide around the field, that becomes more feasible.

We can take a look at that top tranche and say "How many of them showed that they are able to play (first, second, etc.)?" and therefore could have directly substituted for the starter? How many of them could have been a direct substitute for our injured player? We don't know whether one of them would be on *a specific* team, but we can say that 40 percent of the time, a manager would have been able to draw from tranche 1 in filling the role, and 35 percent from tranche 2. But on tranche 1, we can also look at how many of those players played a position that could have then shifted and covered for that spot. We'd need some eligibility criteria for all of this (probably a minimum number of games played) but it would just be a matter of multiplication. Shortstop would be harder to fill, and managers would probably be dipping a little further down in the talent pool, and so replacement level would be lower, as it is now.

Doing some quick analysis, I found that the difference in just batting linear weights (haven't even gotten into running or fielding) between tranche 1 and tranche 2 in 2019 was about 6.5 runs, prorated across 650 PA. Between tranche 1 and tranche 3, it's 10.8 runs. The ability to shift those plate appearances up the ladder has some real value.

This part is important. We can also give credit to starters for the positions that they showed an ability to play, even if they didn't play them (this is the guy fully capable of playing center, but who's in a corner because the team already has a good center fielder) because he allows a team to carry a player who hits like a left fielder to functionally be the team's backup center fielder. He facilitates that movement upward among the tranches. We can start to appreciate the difference between a left fielder who would never be able to hack it in center (and the compensatory move that his team would have to make) and the left fielder who could do it, but just didn't have to very often.

Past that, you can continue to use whatever hitting and fielding and running metrics you like to determine a player's value, but when we get down to constructing that baseline, I'd argue we need a better conceptual and mathematical framework. It's going to require some more #GoryMath than we're used to, but I'd argue it's a better conceptualization of the way that MLB actually plays the game in 2020. If…y'know…MLB plays in 2020. If WAR is going to be our flagship statistic among the *acronymati*, then we need to acknowledge that it contains some old and starting-to-be-out-of-date assumptions about the game. We may need to tinker with it. Here's my idea for how.

—*Russell A. Carleton is an author of Baseball Prospectus.*

Secondhand Sport

by Patrick Dubuque

Back before time stopped, I liked to go to thrift stores. Now that I'm older, I rarely ever buy anything—I don't need much in my life, now—but I still enjoy the old familiar circuit: check to see if there are baseball cards to write about, look for board or card games to play with the kids, scan for random ironic jerseys, hit the book section. It takes ten, maybe fifteen minutes. Thrift stores are the antithesis of modern online shopping, because you don't know what they have, and you don't even really know what you want. It's junk, literal junk, stuff other people thought was worthless. That's what makes it great.

In an idealized economy, thrift stores shouldn't exist. Everybody has a living wage, and every product has a durability that exactly matches its desired life; nothing should need to be given away, no one should need to be given to. But then, thrift stores shouldn't work on a customer experience level, either. You wouldn't think an ethos of "let's make everything disorganized and hard to find" would lead to customer satisfaction, but low-budget retailers like TJ Maxx and Ross thrive on this model. People like bargain hunting as much for the hunting as the bargain; it's part of the experience, spending time as if it's a wager. There's a thrill, occasionally, in inefficiency.

In sports, the modern overuse of the word "inefficiency" is a condemnation: It insinuates that there is *an* efficiency, a correct way to be found, and that all other ways are wrong ways. It's prevalent in baseball but hardly contained to it; the lifehack, the Silicon Valley disruption are other examples of productivity creep in our daily lives. Their modern success makes plenty of sense. Maximization of resources, after all, is its own puzzle, and an industry of European board games is founded upon it. It's fun to take a system and optimize it, unravel it like a sudoku puzzle. If there's only one kind of genius, after all, there's no way anyone can fail to appreciate it.

Baseball has been hacking away at these perceived inefficiencies since its inception: platoons, bullpens, farm systems were all installed to extract more out of the tools at hand. But it's been a particular badge of the sabermetric movement, from Ken Phelps and his All-Star Team to Ricardo Rincon and the darlings of *Moneyball*. It's business, but it's also an ethos: the idea that there's treasure among the trash, something we all failed to appreciate until someone brought it to light.

It's the myth that made Sidd Finch so enticing, that fuels so many "best shape" narratives and new pitch promises. We all, athletes and unathletic sportswriters, want to believe that there's genius trapped inside us, and that it's just a matter of puzzling out the combination to unlock it. That our art, our style is the next inefficiency, waiting for our own Billy Beane. It's why we root for underdogs, and why we're excited for the Mike Tauchmans and the Eurubiel Durazos, champions of skin-deep mediocrity.

Except we aren't anymore, really. The days of "Free X" have descended beyond the ring of irony and into obscurity. There are still Xs to be freed, or at least one X, duplicated endlessly: Mike Ford, Luke Voit, Max Muncy. The undervalued one-dimensional slugger demonstrated how the game hasn't quite culturally caught up to its logical extreme. But for those who don't fit the rather spacious mold, times are grimmer. As Rob Arthur revealed several months ago, there's been a marked increase in the number of sub-replacement relievers. It's the outcome of a greater number of teams forced to play out games without the talent to win them, but it's also emblematic of the modern tendency of teams to dispose of their disposable assets, burning through cost-controlled arms the way that man chopped down forests in *The Lorax*. Stuff just isn't built to outlive their original owners anymore.

It's unsurprising, given how well-mined the market for inefficiencies has been of late. The disciples of the early analytics departments, and the disciples of those, have proliferated the league, with only a few backwater holdouts. The league has grown smarter, but every team has learned the same lesson. In fact, the phenomenon creates a peculiar kind of feedback loop: As teams value a specific subset of players or skills, prospective athletes learn to increase their own marketability by conforming themselves to the demands of their prospective employers.

And that's tragic, in the way that the extinction of animals is tragic; a certain amount of biodiversity in baseball has been lost. Shortstops hit like outfielders. Pitchers don't hit at all. Only the catchers remain idiosyncratic, thanks to the defensive demands of their position; eventually they too will be required to produce like everyone else, or they'll meet the fate of their battery mates. A perfect economy requires perfect production.

I mentioned earlier that more and more, I leave thrift stores empty-handed. It is true that I am more discerning than in the past; my bookshelves are full, and there are more streaming films than I will ever be able to watch. But there are other factors at play.

Thrift stores are, in a way, the bond markets of retail. When the economy is rough and other retailers are struggling, more people look secondhand for their products. But as recently as last year, publications were noting a reversal of the trend: Companies like Goodwill and Savers were expanding despite a strong economy. Publications credited a heightened sense of environmentalism and a rejection of cutting-edge fashion as drivers behind the increase, though the more likely answer is the modern American economy hasn't showered its favors equally, particularly among the young.

But it is more than just the economy. Baseball and thrift stores share something else in common, evident in our current conversations about re-starting the sport: They live in the gray area between public service and private enterprise. Thrift stores provide affordable necessities to lower-class citizens, and collectibles and fashion for the middle-class. Because of the success of the latter, prices have gone up across the board. Especially in terms of clothing, the middle-class flight from fashion into vintage has instead carried the aftereffects of fashion, including its costs, into a territory where people just want clothes. But there's another factor in the rise of prices, in the form of the internet.

The Goodwills of the world have grown smarter, too, employing the internet to extract full value from their detritus. Ebay, similarly, has lost much of the charm it had as a new frontier around the turn of the century. Everything has a price point now; even individual taste is no match for the algorithm, because anything rare, no matter how niche its market, is a collectible to someone.

The internet has had the same effect on thrift stores that sabermetrics has had on baseball; its equivalent to OBP was the bar scanner. As detailed in Slate, the rise of second-party stores on eBay and Amazon birthed an entire industry of used-good salespeople, armed with PDAs and scanners, buying books for three dollars to sell online for five. The author, Michael Savitz, reports earning $60,000 by working nearly 80 hours a week; he makes it clear that this is not a vocation of his choosing. It's long hours, with no real creativity or individuality, skimming the cream off of a local establishment and flipping it to someone with a little more money on the other side of the country. And once the vocation exists, the obvious question arises: why wait to put the wares out on the shelves? Why allow value to exist at all?

Nothing is ruined. Thrift stores will continue to sell polo shirts and DVDs, and baseball will continue to exist and make or lose money, depending on who you believe. But as we continue to refine our knowledge, we lose something in the conquest for efficiency, a delight born out of the unknown. The problem isn't the efficiency itself; we can't blame the booksellers, or the people sweeping freeways to collect grams of platinum from damaged catalytic converters. The problem is a system that requires this sort of profit-skimming behavior in order to feed families (or, for corporations, maximize shareholder return).

Chicago Cubs 2021

In times like these, with the 2020 season on the brink and the collective bargaining agreement close behind, it can often feel like the current situation is untenable. It can't keep going like this, even if we don't know what to do about it. But as with thrift stores, there's an equally irresistible feeling that it *has* to keep going, that it would be unimaginable to not have this broken, amazing sport. Both industries exist on an invisible foundation of friction, of chaos and unpredictability, even as both see their foundations buffed down to a perfect, untouchable polish. But if COVID-19 and its financial ramifications do, as some have suggested, make it such that the baseball that returns is fundamentally different than the baseball that came before, perhaps this is the time to lean in, and change the game even more. Fix bunting. Make defense more difficult. Create viable, alternate strategies. Add some chaos back into baseball. It's fun when no one knows quite where things are.

—Patrick Dubuque is an author of Baseball Prospectus.

Steve Dalkowski Dreaming

by Steven Goldman

We dream of being a pitcher, of starring in the major leagues. Depending on your age and your sense of historical perspective, you might imagine yourself as Walter Johnson, throwing harder than anyone else—hitting more batters than anyone else, too, but always feeling bad about it. You could picture yourself as a Tom Seaver or a David Cone, with all the stuff in the world but still being cerebral about it, thinking about so much more than burning 'em in there. There are so many models one could choose: You could be a Lefty Gomez, Jim Bouton, or Bill Lee, skilled, but not taking the whole thing too seriously, or a Lefty Grove, Bob Gibson, or Steve Carlton, powerful but treating each start like a mission to be survived instead of a game to be enjoyed.

Very few would dream of being Steve Dalkowski, the former Baltimore Orioles prospect who died of COVID-19 last week at the age of 80. Yet, there is something just as noble in Dalkowski's negative accomplishments—and accomplishments is what they are—as there is in the precision-engineered pitching of a Greg Maddux. You have to be very good to be that bad. Dalkowski had all of the stuff of the greatest pitchers but none of the command; his story is not one of failing to conquer his limitations, but striving against one of the cruelest hands that fate or genetics or personality can deal us: A desire to achieve great things which is almost but not quite matched by the ability to meet that goal.

As with Johnson, Grove, Bob Feller, and the rest of the hard-throwing pitchers who played before the advent of modern radar guns, we have to take the word of the players and coaches who saw Dalkowski pitch as to his velocity. He was a hard-drinking, maximum-effort pitcher who, if their memories are to be believed, consistently threw over 100 miles per hour. His was the Maltese Fastball, the stuff that dreams are made of. The problem is that velocity without command and control is still a good distance from utility. Dalkowski was the most effective towel you could design for a fish, the sleekest bathing suit intended to be worn by an astronaut, but that doesn't mean he wasn't beautiful: We can appreciate a journey even if it doesn't end at the intended destination.

Whether because of sloppy mechanics he couldn't calm, an inability to understand that a consistent 98 in the strike zone would likely be more effective than a consistent 110 out of it, or all that beer, Dalkowski could never make the adjustments that pitchers like Feller and Nolan Ryan made before him, possibly because he had so far to go: Feller, who never pitched in the minors, came up at 17 and spent three years walking almost seven batters per nine innings before settling in at 3.8 beginning when he was 20. Ryan started out walking over six batters per nine but gradually improved as his long career played out; for him to go from 6.2 walks per nine with the 1966 Greenville Mets to 3.7 with the 1989 Texas Rangers represents a 40 percent reduction. An equivalent improvement by Dalkowski would still have left him walking over 11 batters per nine innings.

Dalkowski was like *The Room* of pitchers, a player so bad he became good again. Cal Ripken, Sr., who both played with and managed Dalkowski, recalled in a 1979 *Sporting News* "where are they now" piece the occasion when the pitcher crossed up his catcher and his fastball, "hit the plate umpire smack in the mask. The mask broke all to pieces and the umpire wound up in the hospital for three days with a concussion. If they ever had a radar gun in those days, I'll bet Dalkowski would have been timed at 110 miles an hour."

Signed by the Orioles out of New Britain High in Connecticut in 1957, Dalkowski was sent to Kingsport in the Appalachian League, where he pitched 62 innings. He allowed only 22 hits in 62 innings, or 3.2 per nine, a number with no equivalent in major league history (though Aroldis Chapman came close in 2014), and also struck out 121 (17.6 per nine) and walked 129 (18.7). He was also charged with 39 wild pitches. That June, one of his fastballs clipped a Dodgers prospect named Bob Beavers and carried away part of his ear. "The first pitch was over the backstop, the second pitch was called a strike, I didn't think it was," Beavers said last year. "The third pitch hit me and knocked me out, so I don't remember much after that. I couldn't get in the sun for a while, and I never did play baseball again." Former minor leaguer Ron Shelton based the *Bull Durham* pitcher Nuke LaLoosh on Dalkowski. And yet, to see him as a figure of fun, an amusing loser, is to misunderstand something unique and strange.

Dalkowski kept on posting some of the strangest lines in baseball history. Pitching for the Stockton Ports of the Class C California League in 1960, he struck out 262 and walked 262 in 170 innings. Yet, he did improve, especially after pitching for Earl Weaver at Elmira in 1962. Weaver had previously had Dalkowski at Aberdeen in 1959, but wasn't ready to grapple with him then. This time he was. "I had grown more and more concerned about players with great physical abilities who could not learn to correct certain basic deficiencies no matter how much you instructed or drilled them," he related in his autobiography, *It's What You Learn After You Know It All That Counts*. He got permission from the Orioles to give all of his players the Stanford-Binet IQ test. "Dalkowski finished in the 1 percentile in his ability to understand facts. Steve, it was said to say, had the ability to do everything but learn." [sic]

IQ tests are problematic diagnostic tools, so take Weaver's estimate of Dalkowski's mental capabilities with a grain of salt. What's important is that even if he got to the right answer by way of the wrong reason, Weaver had learned something valuable. His insight was to stop asking Dalkowski to learn new pitches and just let him get by with the two that he had. Were Dalkowski a prospect today, that would have been a no-brainer: Can't develop a third pitch? The bullpen is right over there, sir. Player development wasn't like that then, but Weaver, temporarily Dalkowski's mentor, could let him work with what he had. According to Weaver, the pitcher responded: "In the final 57 innings he pitched that season Dalkowski gave up 1 earned run, struck out 110 batters, and walked only 11." It's not true—as per the *Elmira Star-Gazette*, as of late July, Dalkowski had walked 71 in 106 innings and finished with 114 in 160 innings, which means Dalkowski's control actually faded at the end of the season rather than improved—but that doesn't mean it didn't happen in some sense, just that it didn't happen that way. Again, it's the journey, not the destination, and his ERA was 3.04 so *something* had gone right.

Also along the way: The next spring, Orioles manager Billy Hitchcock was rooting for Dalkowski to make the team as a long-man—maybe Weaver had gotten through to him. There were things out of Weaver's control, like the universe's twisted sense of humor: that March, Dalkowski's elbow went "twang."

You sometimes read that it was the Orioles' insistence on Dalkowski learning the curve that did him in, but even if they hadn't learned their lesson, the injury was probably just a coincidence: Dalkowski had thrown an incredible number of pitches over the previous few years. Still, it testifies to the dangers of trying to get what you want and risking the loss of what you had. Dalkowski tried to come back, but the 110-mph stuff was gone. A pitcher with no control and no stuff is…a civilian. What followed were years of vagabond living, arrests for drunkenness. There were Alcoholics Anonymous meetings, assistance from baseball alumni associations, but none of it took. From the 1990s until the time of his passing he dwelt in an assisted living facility, suffering from alcohol-related dementia. He'd been a heavy drinker since his teenage years. As with all those pitches per game, there was a price to be paid. You make choices on the journey and some of them are irrevocable. It's like a fairy tale: "Bite of poison apple? Don't mind if I do."

In the aforementioned *Sporting News* profile, Chuck Stevens, the head of the Association of Professional Ballplayers of America, a ballplayer charity, said, "I've got nothing against drinking. I do it myself sometimes. But, I don't condone common drunkenness. We went through lots of heartache and many dollars, but Dalkowski didn't want to help himself and we weren't going to keep him drunk." The journey is *un*like a fairy tale: No one will come along and kiss it better, not if they're busy forming judgments.

In the end, we are left with a sort of philosophical chicken/egg conundrum: Is failing to meet your goals evidence of unfulfilled potential or the lack of it? Isn't what you did by definition what you were capable of doing? Or could you have broken through to something better with the right help, the right lucky break? These are unanswerable questions, and how we try to answer them may say more about us than about the people we're judging.

No pitcher ever has it easy. *All* pitchers must work hard. *All* pitchers must refine their craft. It's almost never just about *stuff*. Dalkowski dreaming is no insult to the great pitchers who made it; from Pete Alexander to Max Scherzer, they have all earned their way up. And yet, if it is true that we can only do as much as we can do, then the journey would be more of an adventure, the ultimate triumph or defeat more noble, if like Dalkowski we lacked 100 percent of the confidence, the command, the self-possession, the commitment, the resistance to making bad decisions that so many great players possess—to be gloriously human. Or, to put it more succinctly, it would be fun to be able to throw as hard as any person ever has. Even if just for a moment, and even if nothing more came of it than that, no one could say you hadn't lived life to the fullest.

—*Steven Goldman is an author of Baseball Prospectus.*

A Reward For A Functioning Society

by Cory Frontin and Craig Goldstein

On July 5, Nationals reliever Sean Doolittle said in the middle of a press conference regarding the restart of Major League Baseball and what would later be known as summer camp, "sports are like the reward of a functioning society." This sentence was amidst a much longer, thoughtful reply about the societal and health conditions under which MLB players were being brought back. It's a very similar sentiment to one Jane McManus used on April 7, when she discussed the White House's meeting with sports commissioners. She said "sports are the effect of a functioning society—not the precursor."

Both versions of the same sentiment spoke to a laudable ideal in the context of a country that was not addressing a rampaging virus, and opting instead to bring sports back for the feeling of normalcy rather than the reality of it. "Priorities," as McManus said.

On Wednesday, the NBA's Milwaukee Bucks conducted a wildcat/political strike, refusing to come out for Game 5 of their playoff series against the Orlando Magic. The Magic refused to accept the forfeit, and shortly thereafter other playoff series were threatened by player strikes. Eventually the league moved to postpone that day's games, folding to players leveraging their united power.

The backdrop against which these actions took place was the shooting by police of Jacob Blake. Blake was shot in the back seven times by police, as he attempted to get into his vehicle. He managed to survive the assault, but is paralyzed from the waist down.

⚾   ⚾   ⚾

The step taken to walk out, first by the Milwaukee Bucks, then subsequently by other NBA, WNBA, and MLB teams, was a step toward upholding the virtue of the sentiment described by McManus and Doolittle. But that sentiment does not align with the broad history of sports in this and other countries, a history that contradicts the core of the idealistic statement.

Sports have been a significant part of American society for most of its existence, expanding in importance and influence in recent years. The idea that society was functioning in a way that was worthy of the reward of sports for most of that time is laughable. Much of America is not functioning and has not functioned for Black people, full stop. The oppressed people at the center of this political act by players, specifically Black players, in concert throughout the NBA and in fits and starts throughout Major League Baseball, have not known a society that functions for them rather than *because* of them.

Politics has been part of the sports landscape since the inception of sport, but for just about as long people have bemoaned its presence. Sports are to be an escape, it is said. An escape from what, though? A functioning society?

No, the presence of sports has never signified a cultural or political system that is on the up and up. Rather, the presence of sports *reflect and reinforce the society that produces them.*

⚾   ⚾   ⚾

The Negro Leagues were born out of societal dysfunction. The need for entirely separate leagues, composed of Black and Latino players barred from the Major Leagues because of racism? That is not a functioning society, and yet there were sports.

Even the integration of players from the Negro Leagues resulted in a transfer of power and wealth from Black-owned businesses and communities and into white ones, mirroring the dysfunction that had bled into every aspect of American society at the time. Japheth Knopp noted in the Spring 2016 Baseball Research Journal:

> *The manner in which integration in baseball—and in American businesses generally—occurred was not the only model which was possible. It was likely not even the best approach available, but rather served the needs of those in already privileged positions who were able to control not only the manner in which desegregation occurred, but the public perception of it as well in order to exploit the situation for financial gain. Indeed, the very word integration may not be the most applicable in this context because what actually transpired was not so much the fair and equitable combination of two subcultures into one equal and more homogenous group, but rather the reluctant allowance—under certain preconditions—for African Americans to be assimilated into white society.*

To understand the value of a movement, though, is not to understand how it is co-opted by ownership, but to know the people it brings together and what they demand. When Jackie Robinson—the player who demarcated the inevitability of the end of the Negro leagues—attended the March on Washington for Jobs and Freedom in 1963, he did so with his family and marched alongside the people. He stood alongside hundreds of thousands to fight for their common civil and labor rights. "The moral arc of the universe is long," many freedom fighters have echoed, "but it bends towards justice." The bend, it is less frequently said, happens when a great mass of people place the moral arc of the universe on their knee and apply force, as Jackie, his family, and thousands of others did that day.

⚾ ⚾ ⚾

Of course, taking the moral arc of the universe down from the mantle and bending it is not without risk. Perhaps the outsized influence of athletes is itself a mark of a dysfunctional society, but, nonetheless, hundreds of athletes woke up on Wednesday morning with the power to bring in millions of dollars in revenues. That very power, as we would come to find out, was matched with the equal and opposite power to *not* bring those revenues. That power, in hands ranging from the Milwaukee Bucks, to Kenny Smith in the *Inside the NBA* Studio, from the unexpected ally, Josh Hader, and his largely white teammates to the notably Black Seattle Mariners, would be exercised for a single demand: the end to state violence against Black people. Not unlike the March itself, it sat at the intersection of the civil rights of Black Americans and bold labor action. The March on Washington stood in the face of a false notion of integration—against an integration of extraction but not one of equality—and proposed something different. Just the same, the acts of solidarity of August 26, 2020 will be remembered in stark defiance of MLB's BLM-branded, but ultimately empty displays on opening weekend.

Bold defiance like this can never be without risk. By choosing to exercise this power, the Milwaukee Bucks took a risk. They risked vitriol and backlash from those they disagreed with. They risked fines or seeing their contracts voided, as a walkout like this is prohibited by their CBA. They risked forfeiting a playoff game, one that, as the No. 1 seed in the playoffs, they'd worked all year to attain. They didn't know how Orlando would respond. It wasn't clear that other teams throughout the league would follow suit in solidarity. And it wasn't known the league would accept these actions and moderately co-opt them by "postponing" games that would have featured no players.

If the league reschedules the games, some of the athletes' risk—their shared sacrifice—will be diminished, in retrospect. But they did not know any of that when they took that risk. And it is often left to athletes to take these risks when others in society won't, especially those of their same socioeconomic status and levels of influence.

It is athletes, specifically BIPOC athletes, that take them, though, because they live with the risk of being something other than white in this country every day. They are no strangers to the realities of police brutality. It seems incongruous

Chicago Cubs 2021

then, to say that sports are a reward for a functioning society when we rely on athletes to lead us closer to being a functioning society. Luckily, our beloved athletes, WNBA players first and foremost among them, understand what sports truly are: a pipebender for the moral arc of the universe.

—Craig Goldstein is editor in chief of Baseball Prospectus. Cory Frontin is an author of Baseball Prospectus.

Index of Names

Abbott, Cory 80
Adam, Jason 40
Alcántara, Sergio 74
Alzolay, Adbert 42, 90
Amaya, Miguel 75, 89
Báez, Javier 14
Biagini, Joe 81
Bote, David 16
Brothers, Rex 81
Bryant, Kris 18
Carraway, Burl 82, 92
Chafin, Andrew 44
Contreras, Willson 20
Davies, Zach 46
Davis, Brennen 75, 87
Descalso, Daniel 76
Ervin, Phillip 22
Franklin, Kohl 91
Happ, Ian 24
Hendricks, Kyle 48
Heyward, Jason 26
Hoerner, Nico 28
Holder, Jonathan 50
Howard, Ed 76, 88
Jeffress, Jeremy 52
Jensen, Ryan 82, 91
Kimbrel, Craig 54
Little, Luke 93
Machado, Dixon 77
Maples, Dillon 83
Marquez, Brailyn 84, 87
Maybin, Cameron 30
Mills, Alec 56
Morel, Christopher 90
Morel, Rafael 93
Morgan, Adam 58
Nwogu, Jordan 93
Pederson, Joc 32
Phegley, Josh 77
Pinango, Yohendrick 92
Ramos, Heliot 78
Rea, Colin 60
Rizzo, Anthony 34
Roederer, Cole 79
Romine, Austin 36
Russell, Addison 79
Ryan, Kyle 62
Steele, Justin 85
Strumpf, Chase 80
Tepera, Ryan 64
Underwood Jr., Duane 66
Vargas, Ildemaro 38
Wick, Rowan 68
Wieck, Brad 86
Williams, Trevor 70
Winkler, Dan 72

For the Joy of Keeping Score

THIRTY81 Project is an ongoing graphic design project focused on the ballparks of baseball. Since being established in 2013, scorecards have been a fundemantal part of the effort. Each two-page card is uniquely ballpark-centric — there are 30 variants — and designed with both beginning and veteran scorekeepers in mind. Evolving over the years with suggestions from fans, broadcasters, and official scorers, the sheets are freely available to everyone as printable letter-size PDFs at the project webshop. www.THIRTY81Project.com

Download, Print, Score, Repeat ...

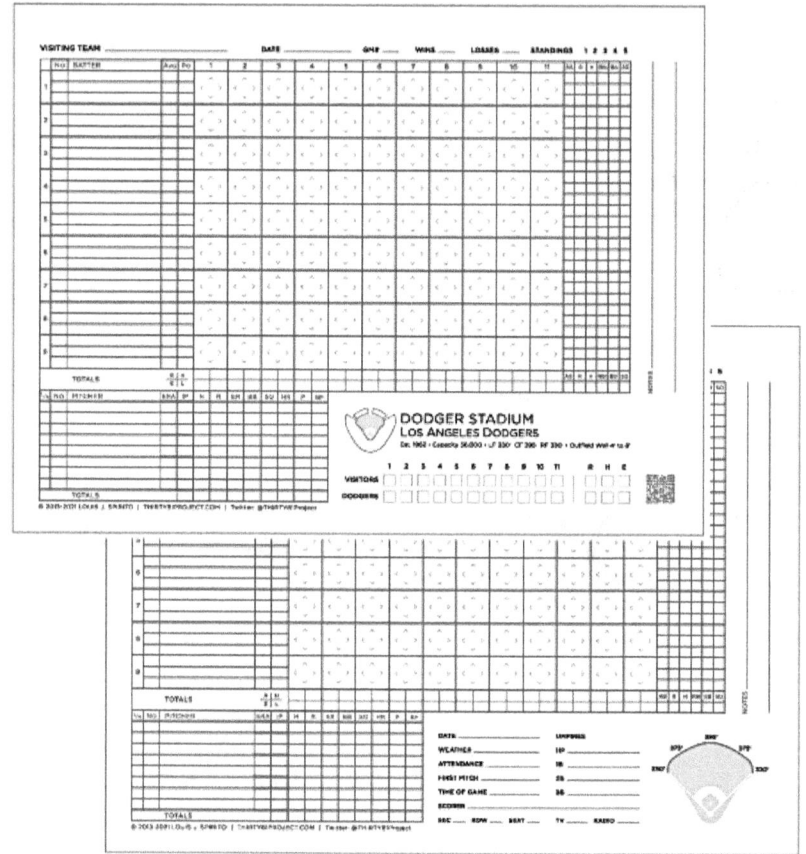

Scorecard design ©2013-2021 Louis J. Spirito | THIRTY81Project